MCR

CULTURES OF THE WORLD
Kuwait

Cavendish
Square
New York

Published in 2019 by Cavendish Square Publishing, LLC
243 5th Avenue, Suite 136, New York, NY 10016
Copyright © 2019 by Cavendish Square Publishing, LLC

Third Edition

This publication represents the opinions and views of the author based on his or her personal experience, knowledge, and research. The information in this book serves as a general guide only. The author and publisher have used their best efforts in preparing this book and disclaim liability rising directly or indirectly from the use and application of this book.
CPSIA Compliance Information: Batch #WS14CSQ
All websites were available and accurate when this book was sent to press.

Library of Congress Cataloging-in-Publication Data

Names: O'Shea, Maria, author. | Spilling, Michael, author. | Nevins, Debbie, author.
Title: Kuwait / Maria O'Shea, Michael Spilling, Debbie Nevins.
Description: Third edition. | New York : Cavendish Square, 2018. | Series: Cultures of the world | Includes bibliographical references and index. |
Audience: 6 & up.
Identifiers: LCCN 2018008907 (print) | LCCN 2018011229 (ebook) | ISBN 9781502636416 (ebook) | ISBN 9781502636409¬ (library bound)
Subjects: LCSH: Kuwait--Juvenile literature.
Classification: LCC DS247.K8 (ebook) | LCC DS247.K8 O7 2018 (print) | DDC 953.67--dc23
LC record available at https://lccn.loc.gov/2018008907

Writers, Maria O' Shea and Michael Spilling; Debbie Nevins, third edition
Editorial Director, third edition: David McNamara
Editor, third edition: Debbie Nevins
Art Director, third edition: Amy Greenan
Designer, third edition: Jessica Nevins
Picture Researcher, third edition: Jessica Nevins
Printed in the United States of America

PICTURE CREDITS

PRECEDING PAGE
The Kuwait Towers are the best known landmark of Kuwait City.

Printed in the United States of America

CONTENTS

KUWAIT TODAY

AT FIRST GLANCE, KUWAIT DOESN'T SEEM LIKE THE SORT OF place with much to offer. It's a small, flat, dry chunk of land in the Middle East—a politically volatile part of the world—on the Arabian Peninsula, itself an environmentally harsh and forbidding place.

Slightly smaller than the state of New Jersey, Kuwait is mostly desert with very little fertile soil for agriculture or forests. It has long, intensely hot summers and is prone to sandstorms and dust storms. Worst of all, it has almost no fresh water—no permanent rivers—and nowhere near enough drinkable water to support its population.

So at first glance, Kuwait hardly seems like a place worth fighting over, though it has been. And it certainly doesn't seem like the sort of place that would be one of the wealthiest nations on earth. But it is.

To be sure, one of Kuwait's great assets is its 310-mile (499-kilometer) coastline at the head of the Persian Gulf (sometimes called the Arabian Gulf). In earlier days, one of its main natural resources was pearls from the oysters on the bottom of the

A derrick (oil pump) operates in a Kuwait oil field near the Saudi Arabian border.

sea. But today, the main source of Kuwait's fabulous riches can be summed up in one word—oil.

Beneath that arid landscape lies a treasure trove of oil, and it has made all the difference. What was once, in ancient times, a prosperous trading port, which had descended into poverty by the early twentieth century, has become a modern state. The capital, Kuwait City, is an oasis of modern technology, full of museums, restaurants, modern shopping complexes, international hotels, and luxury beach resorts.

One thing that hasn't changed in Kuwait is the man at the top—the individual changes but he is always, by law, a member of the Al-Sabah family. The dynasty has ruled the country since 1756. At this writing, the emir is Sabah Al-Ahmad Al-Jaber Al-Sabah (b. 1929), one of the world's oldest (by age) heads of state. Another thing that has remained the same is its Arab identity, and Islam, the country's official religion. Indeed, Arab-Islamic identity, language, and culture, along with oil-derived wealth, are the defining characteristics of Kuwaiti society. Although the country shares much of its lifestyle with its Gulf neighbors, it has forged an identity of its own built around the ruling emir and careful investment of its oil wealth in public projects.

Kuwait is so rich that its citizens don't really have to work. They are supported by the government, rather than the other way around. Kuwaitis receive a comfortable monthly stipend and pay no taxes. Although many have jobs in upper-level government positions, the country imports people— expatriates from other nations—to do much of the work, in both highly-specialized professional fields and low-paid, low-status labor.

Most Kuwaiti households have domestic workers—maids, cooks, nannies, gardeners—who tend to come from less-affluent Middle Eastern and Asian nations. Indians, Egyptians, Pakistanis, and Syrians make up a large number of the foreigners working in Kuwait. Some of the lowest level jobs, however, are taken by Filipinos. Some 60 percent of them are employed as domestic workers, and most send money back home to their families in the Philippines.

However, many domestic workers have complained about abuse at the hands of their Kuwaiti employers. They work very few legal protections. Sometimes, employers take possession of the workers' passports to prevent them from leaving. The workers may then be overworked, unpaid, starved, beaten, or sexually abused. Sometimes they are even killed.

The issue came to head in 2018 when the body of a Filipino maid was discovered in an apartment in Kuwait. She had been tortured and murdered, presumably by her employers, who had fled. The Philippine president Rodrigo Duterte responded angrily by banning Filipinos from working in Kuwait and offering free flights home for those who wished to return. The Philippine ambassador to Kuwait said he had received almost six thousand complaints of abuse in the previous year.

The issue reflects poorly on Kuwaitis; but then, of course not all Kuwaitis abuse their domestic help. However, the problem appears to be a symptom of a culture of great wealth with little accountability. On the one hand, Kuwaitis want foreigners to do their grunt work for them. But now

The Constitution Monument in Kuwait City's Al Shaheed Park, shown here lit up at night, commemorates the fiftieth anniversary of the constitution's ratification.

The lights of the architecturally impressive Sheik Jaber Al Ahmad Cultural Center reflect in the water in Kuwait City.

that the population of expats outnumbers the Kuwaiti nationals themselves, the citizens resent the foreigners and want them to leave. Though Kuwaitis are willing to pick up some of the more elite, professional jobs being performed by foreigners, they certainly wouldn't be willing to do the lower-status jobs.

With great wealth often comes great power, along with feelings of entitlement and superiority—even though the source of the wealth may have nothing whatsoever to do with the individual's own accomplishments. Kuwaiti citizens are rich because there is oil under their soil, and their leaders have made wise investments in their society, infrastructure, and future.

They have good reason to be proud of their gleaming cities with their cultural attractions and astonishing architecture. They are rightly proud of their technological achievements—not least of which are the state-of-the-art desalination stations that turn seawater into enough potable water to support the Kuwaiti's record-breaking water usage.

Kuwaitis value their independence, and were profoundly threatened by the invasion of their much bigger neighbor Iraq in 1990—1991. The United States played the major role in defending the small country in what came to be called "the Gulf War," and Iraq's forces were driven out. That support cemented Kuwait—US relations, at least for the time being. Today, that alliance holds, but in general, relations between the broader Arab world and the West are strained by numerous issues.

Kuwait today faces several challenges. Political tensions between Islamic fundamentalists, moderates, and progressives are running high. Finding the balance between deeply-rooted Islamic values and the modern world is a task fraught with fierce emotions and diverse perspectives. Different groups have distinct visions for how they think Kuwaiti society should function, with rights and freedoms being the main sticking points. Issues of women's rights, press and media freedom, political openness, corruption, cause frictions that will not be easily solved. The "Kuwaitization" of the labor force—a trend now underway—will create a new population profile, even as citizens are asked to shoulder more of the responsibility of doing the work of the nation.

A solar power station in Kuwait

And what of all that oil? Slowly, Kuwaitis are coming to grips with the idea that the oil in the ground won't last forever, and neither will the international demand for it. Slowly, the country is realizing the need to diversify its economy, and even its power sources. In 2016, Kuwait's first-ever solar power plant went online. And in 2018, the government approved the building of another big solar-power plant as part of its plan to produce about 15 percent of its power from renewable resources by 2030. The future seems bright for Kuwait.

GEOGRAPHY

A dromedary, or Arabian camel, walks through the sandy desert.

1

KUWAIT IS A VERY SMALL COUNTRY surrounded by much larger neighbors. Squeezed between the vast kingdom of Saudi Arabia and the large country of Iraq, tiny Kuwait extends 124 miles (200 km) north to south and 106 miles (170 km) east to west. On the east, Kuwait has coastline on the Persian Gulf.

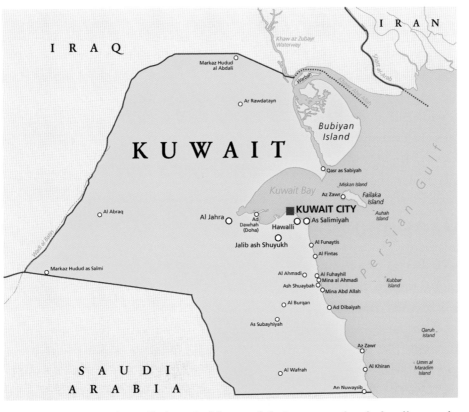

This map of Kuwait shows that most of its populated areas are located on the coast.

Kuwait has nine islands, of which the most important ones, in terms of oil reserves and archaeological sites, are Bubiyan and Failaka.

DESERT AND SEASHORE

Kuwait can be divided into four geographic zones: the desert plateau in the west; a desert plain, covering most of the country; salt marshes and saline depressions that cover most of Kuwait Bay; and an eastern area of coastal dunes. The country consists of a gently undulating desert that gradually rises away from the sea to a maximum height of 475 feet (145 meters) in the northwest and 951 feet (290 m) in the east.

Kuwait Bay is one of two generous-size natural harbors in the northern half of the Gulf; the other is in Bahrain. It has always been a prime access point for trade entering and leaving the hinterland of northeast Saudi Arabia and Iraq. Before oil was discovered, the bay was Kuwait's most valuable resource, and as the location of the country's main commercial port, its economic importance continues.

The terrain varies from firm clay and gravel in the north to loose, sandy soil in the south. The plain is an arid steppe desert, and except in the northeast, there are few sand dunes. There are no rivers, lakes, or mountains, but the flatness is relieved by shallow depressions and a few low hills, such as Ahmadi Hill at 450 feet (137 m) in the south and Jal Az-Zor Ridge at 476 feet (145 m) on the north side of Kuwait Bay. The coastline in the north and around Kuwait Bay consists mainly of mudflats, while there are many fine beaches in the south.

NOMADS AND BORDERS

As there are no mountains, rivers, or other natural obstacles, Kuwait was for a long time a transit area for nomadic tribes known as the Bedouin, whose caravans moved freely over the desert. This made it difficult to agree on the boundaries separating the countries in the area. There was much dispute over this, resulting—much later—in boundary problems with Saudi Arabia and Iraq.

WHAT'S IN A NAME?

The Persian Gulf separates Kuwait and the other Arab gulf states from Iran (also known by its historic name Persia). But more than just water separates these longtime adversaries—political and religious differences have long caused conflict between them. The gulf is an extension of the Arabian Sea, and for the last half century or so, Arabs have chosen to call this body of water the Arabian Gulf. Iranians, for their part, strongly object to the renaming of the gulf, which has been named for Persia since ancient times. So which is it, the Persian Gulf or the Arabian Gulf? There's no answer that pleases everyone.

For diplomats and other foreign entities, this political name game can be a very touchy one. The US State Department calls it the Persian Gulf (though US Navy fleets based in the region use Arabian Gulf); the UN uses Persian Gulf; National Geographic and Google Maps show both terms, with Arabian Gulf in parentheses. However, Google will show either Arabian or Persian Gulf to local users, depending on their location and language settings.

Attempts at defusing the controversy by diplomatically calling that body of water "The Gulf" have mostly failed in their good intentions—causing anger on both sides, which find even neutrality to be an affront.

In 1922 the British negotiated an agreement on the Kuwaiti—Saudi Arabia border. This led to the creation of a compromise neutral zone, which was formally divided between the two countries in 1969. Kuwait's northern border with Iraq was agreed upon in 1923, but Iraqi claims on Kuwaiti territory continued: first in 1938, the year oil was discovered in Kuwait, and again in 1961, when Britain recognized Kuwait's independence.

CLIMATE AND WEATHER

The climate of Kuwait is typical of the desert regions but is modified by its coastline, which is 310 miles (499 km) long. Summers are long, hot, and dry, with a daily average temperature of 110° Fahrenheit (43° Celsius). Winters are short and cool, occasionally cold, with rare sudden showers and dust storms. During fall, temperatures start to decrease to the lower 80s°F (28°C) throughout October and the upper to mid-60s°F (20°C) in November. During the winter months, from November to February, the average temperature is 55°F (13°C). Even at this time of year, daytime temperatures can rise to 80°F (27°C), although they can drop as low as 35°F (2°C) if there is night frost. In the spring months, clouds build up throughout the afternoons seemingly from nowhere, bringing occasional thunderstorms by the evening. Directional winds are seasonal: hot and dry from the north, and warm and humid from the south.

Rainfall is unpredictable, from as little as 0.8 inch (2 centimeters) in one year to as much as 13.8 inches (35 cm) in another, though the average is less than 3.2 inches (8 cm) annually. Dust storms occur throughout the year but are more common in the spring and summer. Humidity is usually low, except in the late summer. The highest recorded temperature was 125°F (52°C) in July 1978, making Kuwait the fourth hottest place in the world, and the lowest was 25°F (-4°C) in January 1964. Daily fluctuation is wide, especially in the desert, where the nights can be very cold, even in summer.

SCARCITY OF FRESH WATER

The lack of fresh drinking water has always been a serious problem in Kuwait. There are few naturally occurring water sources. The water is mostly brackish, though it can be used for irrigation and cleaning. Even before the oil era, clean drinking water was imported from Iraq. A good domestic source of drinking water was not discovered until the late 1950s, at al-Rawdatain and Umm al-Aish in the north. This underground reservoir contains possibly 48 billion gallons (182 billion liters) and is the only source of fresh water in the country.

The bulk of Kuwait's water—90 percent—comes from the sea and is processed at desalination plants, all of which are owned and managed by the government. Despite its extremely expensive water situation, Kuwait has the highest water consumption level in the world. Kuwaitis use about 132 gallons (500 liters) per capita per day, more than double the average international rate.

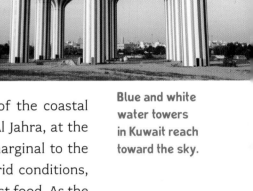

Blue and white water towers in Kuwait reach toward the sky.

WHEN THE DESERT BLOOMS

Although vegetable gardens were once cultivated on parts of the coastal strip, and date palms and fruit trees were once the pride of Al Jahra, at the western end of Kuwait Bay, farming has always been very marginal to the economy. The immense effort involved in farming in such arid conditions, using limited water supplies, means it is cheaper to import most food. As the Kuwaiti government is much concerned about the country's dependence on the outside world, some areas of the desert have been irrigated, and farming is practiced at a great financial cost, notably in Wafra, Sulaibiya, and Abdali.

Plant life in Kuwait is sparse, since there is little regular rain. The soil is mostly sandy and often salty. The desert is scattered with patches of coarse, weedy grass and small bell-shape bushes. The country has up to four hundred types of vegetation, and a good rainfall in winter can produce an abundant growth of lush green grass and wildflowers; these quickly wither and die, however.

Kuwait's national flower is the arfaj flower. The arfaj plant is a bushy shrub with small thorny leaves and bright yellow flowers that grows in the deserts of the Arabian Peninsula.

ANIMAL LIFE

The desert contains many rodents, lizards, and other small animals, but the rabbits, wolves, and gazelles that once roamed the desert have been hunted to near extinction. There is some pasture for sheep, goats, and camels. These

A greater flamingo preens its feathers.

animals may appear to wander wild, but they actually belong to the Bedouin tribes. Although Kuwait has only twenty native species of birds, mostly larks, more than three hundred types of birds pass through in the spring and the fall on their annual migration, using Kuwait as a stop-off point. These include flamingos, steppe eagles, cormorants, and bee-eaters. At certain times of the year, pink flamingos can be seen on the salt flats to the north of Kuwait City.

The waters of the Gulf are very salty and warm, with temperatures ranging from 54°F to 97°F (12°C to 36°C). More than two hundred species of fish and other sea animals can be found in the local waters, including dolphins, porpoises, whales, and sea snakes. Many types of shellfish can be found along the shores of Kuwait, as well as in the beds deep under the sea.

KUWAITI CITIES

More than 90 percent of Kuwait's 2,875,000 people live along a coastal belt about 6 miles (10 km) deep, stretching from Al Jahra at the western edge of Kuwait Bay to Mina Abdullah to the south of Kuwait City, a distance of about 50 miles (80 km). This is known as the metropolitan area.

The rest of Kuwait is only very sparsely populated. In recent years, the Kuwaiti government has built cities in the west, the northeast, and the south to absorb the population increase and to relieve the pressure on the metropolitan area. The population of Kuwait grows by 1.46 percent per year (as of 2017), mostly due to incoming expatriates—foreigners who come to the country for work.

The main cities are Kuwait City, located on the site of the original fort settlement at the southwestern tip of Kuwait Bay; Al Jahra, an old agricultural town to the west; and al-Salmiya, to the east of the bay. These cities and the southern coastal cities of Mina al-Ahmadi and Mina Abdullah are linked and encircled by a network of more than 3,037 miles (4,887 km) of expressways.

About 12 miles (20 km) or so off the coast of Kuwait City lies the nation's only inhabited island. It's not terribly large, measuring about 12 miles (20 km) long by 7.5 miles wide (12 km), and there was a time when it supported a population of about two thousand people. But only a few of those remain today.

During the Iraqi invasion of 1990, most of those residents fled the island for the mainland and they have, for the most part, never come back. Much of the island lies in ruins, its buildings crumbling and scarred with bullet holes. The island's village of Al-Zawr was, until the invasion, the longest continuously inhabited location in Kuwait.

Ruins of another sort are also found on this island, since its history of human occupation dates back to at least 2000 BCE. The vestiges of ancient temples and other antiquities are found here, but have never been properly protected. The Kuwaiti army still uses the island for military exercises.

Life is beginning to return to Failaka Island, as it has become a popular daytrip destination for Kuwaitis. Some are trying to develop a tourist industry on the island, even to the point of envisioning a bridge from the mainland. Until then, ferries run sightseers back and forth.

The total area of the Kuwait City metro area is 77.2 square miles (200 sq km). Only five other populated areas exist outside of the metropolitan area—the oil towns of al-Abdaliya, al-Subayhiyah, and Wafra, and the ports of al-Khiran and Mina Saud, all to the south and west.

KUWAIT CITY The area originally known as Kuwait City, which is the seat of the government, is a small parcel of land, just 1,999 acres (809 hectares), or one-tenth the size of New York's Manhattan Island. The emir's palace and most offices of banks and investment firms are found here. The city and its suburbs have been rebuilt since the 1950s in a series of master plans. The area was zoned into business and residential areas divided by ring roads, which expand outward in concentric circles.

After independence all citizens were granted free housing. The residential areas of Kuwait City were allocated according to tribal, racial, and religious groups. So it is that certain areas are inhabited by Shiite Muslims, others by Sunni Muslims, and still others by Bedouin tribes. The various immigrant communities were also allocated housing in distinct districts. All sixteen residential zones have their own social amenities, such as shopping malls, mosques, libraries, health centers, banks, restaurants, and cafés. This urban lifestyle thus reinforces the tribal, class, racial, and religious divisions that exist in Kuwait.

AL-AHMADI Lying south of Kuwait City, al-Ahmadi was Kuwait's first oil town, founded more than sixty years ago. Although it now lies in the metropolitan area, it is still noted for its greenery, pleasant gardens, and villas on tree-lined avenues. Before Kuwait City's massive expansion and the construction of the expressway, Mina al-Ahmadi was a 45-minute car journey across the desert from the capital. It was a popular place to spend a relaxing day picnicking in the parks. The town was founded by the Kuwait Oil Company, and the green surroundings were considered to be essential for the morale of employees. Today the port acts a major refueling base for US commercial and military shipping.

INTERNET LINKS

http://www.aljazeera.com/indepth/inpictures/2015/08/kuwaiti-island-frozen-time-150803062651180.html
This slide show presents images of Failaka Island.

https://www.britannica.com/place/Kuwait
This online encyclopedia provides a good overview of Kuwait's geography.

HISTORY

2

KUWAIT IS A NEW COUNTRY, HAVING achieved independence from Britain only in 1961. Yet Kuwaitis have a long-standing and well-developed sense of their unique identity. This is partly due to formal attempts by the government to fashion such an identity and also to the nature of the country's past.

Despite its short history Kuwait has always been relatively independent and distinct from its neighbors. Its traditional dependence on trade with the rest of the world and on pearl diving—pearls being a major natural resource—ensured that Kuwaitis were exposed to many cultures.

The trading and seafaring life meant that men could be absent for up to a half-year; those left behind became dependent on each other for support. This created a powerful sense of community, which at least partially survived the oil boom.

Kuwaiti history was one of almost uninterrupted economic success until the Iraqi invasion of 1990. Despite the devastation visited upon Kuwait's oil industry and infrastructure by the invasion, Kuwait has since recovered from the effects of the Iraqi army occupation to become a stable, comfortable, and prosperous country once again.

Up until recent times, Kuwait enjoyed relative peace throughout its history. While the discovery of oil has generated revenue, it has also caused conflict with Kuwait's neighbors.

Wealth generated from trading has given way to wealth from oil and investments, but the same groups of tribes and families have continued to profit. To a large extent Kuwaiti history is also that of certain families who founded the country three hundred years ago and continue to govern it in the face of increasing challenges and growing Western influence.

OLD KUWAIT

Three hundred and fifty years ago, Kuwait City was an uninhabited headland jutting into the northwest corner of the Persian Gulf. The town of Kuwait was built in 1672 by the Bani Khalid, the dominant tribe of northeastern Arabia in the early eighteenth century. It was called Grane until the mid-nineteenth century. Kuwait is a diminutive of the word *kut* (kuht), meaning "castle" or "fort." A scattering of nomadic families lived along the shore with their camels. Internal disputes and waning influence over the region eventually caused the Bani Khalid clan to decline, allowing the Bani Utub people to rise to power.

The Bani Utub tribe, a loosely connected group of interrelated families from central Arabia, arrived in Kuwait in the early eighteenth century. Famine had forced them to migrate in the late seventeenth century, traveling to Kuwait via Qatar. Once settled in Kuwait they lived by pearl diving, boatbuilding, and trading. The settlement became an important port of call for the desert caravans transporting goods from the Persian Gulf to Aleppo in Syria. By the end of the nineteenth century, the town had a population of ten thousand people. A majority of the men were involved in seafaring trades.

KUWAIT DEVELOPS AS A CITY-STATE

By the mid-eighteenth century the al-Sabah family had become Kuwait's political rulers, a position it still holds. Family members were responsible for political functions, such as diplomatic and tribal relations and security, while other families handled economic and trading matters. Kuwait's small size meant that diplomacy and manipulation of local power balances were necessary to keep a degree of independence from the surrounding powers.

ALEXANDER THE GREAT AND KUWAIT

Archaeologists believe that Failaka was a holy island, possibly a place of pilgrimage three thousand years ago for the Sumerians of Mesopotamia, a land that now constitutes the

greater part of Iraq. When Failaka was discovered by one of Alexander the Great's generals, its sanctuary and shrines to Artemis, the goddess of hunting, were noted. The island contains Kuwait's richest archaeological sites, with Greek temples and fortresses and three Bronze Age settlements.

Alexander the Great conquered most of the Middle East before his death at the age of thirty-three in 323 BCE. Greek historians described the many journeys of Alexander the Great and his companions, including the establishment of a garrison on an island in the Persian Gulf named Icarus; this occurred shortly before Alexander's death. From archaeological explorations carried out in the 1960s, it is believed that the Kuwaiti island of Failaka is the legendary island of Icarus. Although Alexander died three days before his planned conquest of Arabia, Icarus remained an outpost of the successor Seleucid kingdom, which was based in Syria. During this time it prospered as a trading center, until it was overrun by the Parthians, becoming part of Persia but ceasing to have any importance.

Thus the al-Sabah family was able to establish a strong power base at the expense of the other tribes. In 1756 the Bani Utub elected Sabah I bin Jaber (Sabah I) as the first emir of Kuwait.

Until World War I, Kuwait, like the rest of the Arabian Peninsula and the Arab world, was part of the Ottoman Empire's sphere of influence, ruled from

Istanbul, Turkey. In the late nineteenth century, the Ottomans added most of the Gulf coastal regions to the province of Basra (in what today is Iraq), including Kuwait in 1871. The al-Sabah agreed to this, despite having ruled Kuwait for 150 years, as long as the ruler was given the title of governor and the al-Sabah were allowed to continue to govern the country.

BRITAIN AND KUWAIT

At about that time, the British became interested in Iraq and the Gulf, as it was an important staging post on the way to India, which was one of the most important parts of the British Empire.

A regular steamship service between Basra and Bombay called at Kuwait, and British Indian postal services were available to traders. British interest in the area provided the Kuwaiti rulers with a way to free themselves of Ottoman control, and in 1899 Sheikh Mubarak al-Sabah signed an agreement with Britain. In return for British protection, Kuwait agreed not to dispose of any part of its territory or enter into any relationship with any power other than Britain. In 1913 the borders of Kuwait, the Arabian region known as Nejd, and the province of Basra were defined. Britain was in control, and the al-Sabah family had to tread carefully to maintain any independence.

During World War I, Kuwait was occupied by British forces, which were fighting against Ottoman Turkey for control of the Middle East. In return the British promised the Kuwaitis an independent state after the war. At the end of the war and with the collapse of the Ottoman Empire, the British and the French divided up the Middle East. Kuwait remained under British rule.

FROM PEARLS TO OIL

Pearls were once Kuwait's main source of income. However, the pearling industry went into a decline in the early part of the twentieth century due to two factors. For one, the Japanese developed a cheap method of artificial pearl cultivation, which created a large quantity of less expensive pearls. And a worldwide economic depression in the 1920s and 1930s caused a dramatic fall in the demand for pearls in Europe and the United States. By 1945 only five pearling boats were still working in Kuwait out of the five hundred boats that were active at the turn of the century.

Just then, oil was discovered in Kuwait in 1938, and would soon replace pearls as Kuwait's greatest treasure. Oil exploitation began in earnest after World War II ended. By 1957 Kuwait was the second-largest oil exporter in the world, exceeded only by Venezuela. As one of the world's least populated countries, with fewer than 250,000 people, Kuwait was set to become one of the wealthiest.

The oil boom was overseen by the emir, Sheikh Abdullah III al-Salim al-Sabah, who died four years after Kuwait's independence in 1961. He transformed the country into a modern state and dramatically improved social conditions.

The British had the sole right to exploit Kuwait's oil until Kuwait became officially independent. During the next thirty years, Kuwait's oil revenues allowed it to rapidly develop into a modern, comfortable Gulf state.

In this photo from 1930, pipes convey oil from Mina-al-Ahmadi harbour in Kuwait to an off-shore jetty to fill oil tankers.

THE BULLY NEXT DOOR

Kuwait had an uncomfortable relationship with its big neighbor Iraq. Under Saddam Hussein, who served as Iraq's president from 1979 to 2003, Iraq considered the international boundaries of the Arab countries to be illegitimate because they had been imposed by the colonialist Europeans. In particular, Saddam felt Kuwait should rightly be part of Iraq, not only because of historic trading links but also because Bedouin tribes had always moved between the two countries before the creation of national boundaries.

From 1980 to 1988, Iraq waged a war against its neighbor on the other side, Iran. After eight years of a damaging and fruitless war, Iraq needed money, and cast its eye on certain oil fields straddling the Iraq-Kuwait boundary. The rights to those fields were unresolved, and Iraq wanted more oil to sell.

Kuwait, meanwhile, had made a lot of oil available on the world market, which caused the price to drop. Iraq had asked Kuwait to reduce the amount of oil it sold in order to raise oil prices, but Kuwait refused. The Kuwaitis also wanted Iraq to repay the loans incurred when Iraq was at war with Iran. Throughout the summer of 1990, Kuwait and Iraq argued about oil production and prices, the disputed oil fields, and loan repayments. As efforts to resolve the dispute foundered, Iraq moved troops and weapons to the Kuwaiti border.

IRAQ INVADES

Saddam Hussein had invaded another country before, in 1980 when Iraq invaded Iran. Officially that had been over a border dispute, and Iraq had received, if not open support, at least no retaliatory action from the United States or the United Nations. That past experience, as well as a conversation with the US ambassador to Iraq, led Hussein to think that another invasion would be the best solution to his problems with Kuwait and would not meet with any serious objection from the United States. Most Iraqis felt Kuwaitis were too wealthy and that they should be forced to share that wealth more.

In the middle of the night on August 2, 1990, Iraqi soldiers and tanks swept into Kuwait. Kuwait's army totaled only 17,000 soldiers with little experience, while the Iraqi army of 1 million soldiers had the experience of almost a decade of war with Iran.

By morning Iraqi troops controlled Kuwait City. The emir of Kuwait and his close family escaped to Saudi Arabia. Despite a UN resolution asking Iraq to withdraw, the Iraqis proclaimed a transitional government. Within a week US troops began to arrive in Saudi Arabia, as it was feared that Iraq would extend its invasion to Saudi Arabia. In response, President Hussein declared Kuwait the nineteenth province of Iraq. Several Arab states joined forces with the United States to set up Operation Desert Shield, involving 250,000 soldiers, including 200,000 Americans. The operations were aimed at defending Saudi Arabia and encouraging Iraq to withdraw peacefully from Kuwait.

Inside Kuwait the civilian population was terrorized, and those who resisted were tortured and executed under a harsh military regime. Economic sanctions against Iraq were not working, and people became even more fearful that Iraq's apparent success in Kuwait would embolden it to attack Saudi Arabia. Allied troop strength in Saudi Arabia was increased to 550,000, including 350,000 Americans, while Iraqi forces in Kuwait rose to 600,000.

By January 1991, a diplomatic solution appeared impossible, so on January 17 the allied forces began Operation Desert Storm—a devastating air campaign against Iraq and occupied Kuwait. On February 24 the ground assault began, and the coalition forces entered both Kuwait and southern Iraq. Within two days the allied troops had reoccupied Kuwait City, and on February 28, after one hundred hours of fighting, a cease-fire was called. Kuwait paid the coalition forces $17 billion for their help.

Destroyed Iraqi vehicles can be seen beside Kuwait's Highway 80, nicknamed the "Highway of Death," after being bombed by coalition forces on February 27-28, 1991.

THE AFTERMATH OF WAR

Many hoped that the end of the war would see a number of changes in the Arab world and the Gulf states, including a greater degree of democracy. Restoring law and order in Kuwait was difficult. Suspected collaborators—especially expatriate Palestinians—were sought out and punished.

Kuwait's infrastructure was badly damaged and looting was widespread. Goods such as hospital equipment, cars, computers, and valuables were carted away to Iraq, as were antiquities from the museums. Very few houses escaped the looting, and most public offices and facilities, such as schools and the university, were stripped of their contents and wrecked. Many buildings were badly damaged, and the desalination plants, which provide most of Kuwait's water, needed to be rebuilt, as did the airport and the harbors. Bomb damage to the oil installations caused a huge oil slick that harmed marine life and the fishing industry. The Iraqis set fire to 600 of the 950 oil wells in the

A Kuwaiti child poses with a tank after the country's liberation from Iraqi occupation.

country; the smoke polluted the whole Gulf region. It took less than a year to extinguish the burning oil wells, but for more than two years, land mines were still being discovered.

Most of the people who had stayed behind during the invasion were those who did not have Kuwaiti citizenship, such as the Palestinians, and were afraid to leave in case they would not be allowed to return. After the war, expatriates who were thought to have collaborated with the Iraqis were summarily expelled or refused reentry. Even those who were not found to be collaborators but who had remained in Kuwait during the occupation came under suspicion and were expelled or deprived of their residency rights. The Palestinians were singled out for harsh treatment because the Palestinian political leadership had supported the Iraqi government. Without the Palestinians, however, Kuwait was deprived of a highly skilled and educated workforce.

After liberation Kuwaitis worked together to restore the country to some degree of normality. More than $5 billion was spent on rebuilding and restoring the country, especially repairing the damage to the oil infrastructure. The elections in 1992 were widely interpreted as a success for the supporters of increased Islamic law. They were a disappointment to liberals, including those who supported extending suffrage to women, who were not to receive that right until 2005.

In 2003 Kuwait served as the major staging base for the US-led invasion of Iraq for the purpose of ousting Saddam Hussein. As a close American ally, Kuwait was the only Arab nation to publicly support the invasion.

After the death of Sheikh Jaber III al-Ahmad al-Jaber al-Sabah in January 2006, the then-prime minister, Sheikh Sabah IV al-Ahmad al-Sabah (b. 1929), was elected emir of Kuwait. He was chosen over his elderly cousin, Sheikh Saad al-Abdullah, who despite being directly in line for the throne was too ill and frail to take up the position.

Since the invasion, Kuwait has grappled primarily with the political tensions between religious conservatives and progressive reformers. Since becoming emir, Sheikh Sabah has maintained Kuwait's pro-Western stance and pursued a policy of cautious reform.

INTERNET LINKS

http://www.bbc.com/news/world-middle-east-14647211
BBC News provides a timeline of important events in Kuwait.

https://www.britannica.com/place/Kuwait/History
The encyclopedia covers the history of Kuwait up through recent events.

https://www.lonelyplanet.com/kuwait/history#155615
Lonely Planet offers a quick overview of Kuwaiti history.

GOVERNMENT

The Kuwaiti flag waves in Kuwait City.

3

Kuwait was the first
Arab Gulf country
to have an elected
parliament, the
National Assembly.

THE STATE OF KUWAIT, OR DAWLAT al-Kuwayt in Arabic, is a constitutional monarchy, ruled by the emir of Kuwait, who by law must be from the al-Sabah family, descended from the late Mubarak al-Sabah (1837—1915).

The emir (sometimes spelled amir) rules with the help of an elected National Assembly, a Council of Ministers selected by the prime minister and approved by the emir, and the bureaucracy. The emir appoints the prime minister. To a large extent, these institutions have been successful in creating a national identity that inspires loyalty to the country's leaders. The government has generally encouraged the people of Kuwait to support the national interest without using force. The government has faced opposition from liberals and Islamists, but disagreements have largely been resolved peacefully.

The process hit a bump during the years 2012—2013. After Islamists scored major gains in the February 2012 parliamentary elections, Emir Sabah al-Ahmad al-Jaber al-Sabah annulled the results, dissolving parliament. He also changed the election law such that voters could vote for only one candidate rather than four, as had been previously allowed. This sparked protests and a boycott of the subsequent election in December 2012, for which turnout was 43 percent, the lowest in the Kuwaiti electoral history. In June 2013, the Constitutional Court ordered the dissolution of the new National Assembly and the holding of fresh elections, in which pro-government Sunni candidates won a significant majority. However, in the 2016 elections, the Islamist opposition again gained seats.

THE CONSTITUTION

The constitution was signed into law in November 1962 and remains the foundation of Kuwait's political and legal systems. It defines Kuwait as "a hereditary Emirate, the succession to which shall be in the descendants of the late Mubarak al-Sabah" and details how the government is to be organized. The constitution also establishes Islam as the country's official religion and Arabic as the official language.

The Emir of Kuwait, Sabah al-Ahmad al-Jaber al-Sabah speaks to the National Assembly in Kuwait City on Dec. 11, 2016.

The document provides for freedom of speech and the press—more so than other Arab countries—but only "in accordance with the conditions and in the circumstances defined by law." Criticism of the emir, Islam, and religious leaders is forbidden, and those restrictions can be quite broadly applied. Penalties can include prison time and fines.

THE HOUSE OF SABAH

Although the al-Sabah family has ruled Kuwait since the eighteenth century, the family has ruled as a formal institution only since the mid-twentieth century. Since independence, the ruling family has always held at least one-quarter of all cabinet posts and the most important ministerial posts such as foreign affairs, defense, information, and the interior. There are more than 1,200 members of the al-Sabah family, who are themselves divided into various groups depending on their closeness to the ruling line, the descendants of the first emir's sons, Jabir and Salim.

THE EMIR

The emir of Kuwait is the head of state. He is nominated by a family council headed by prominent members of the family, pending approval of the parliament. Within one year of his accession to the throne, the reigning emir must appoint an heir apparent, the crown prince. Traditionally, the choice of emir has alternated between the two main branches of the House of Sabah, the al-Ahmed and al-Salim branches. Since 2006, the emir has been Sabah al-Ahmad al-Jabir al-Sabah (b. 1929), who is quite elderly at this writing, and the crown prince is the emir's half brother, Nawaf al-Ahmad al-Jabir al-Sabah (b. 1937), who is not much younger.

THE NATIONAL ASSEMBLY

The National Assembly is considered one of the strongest parliaments in the Gulf today, and its members sometimes express robust differences of opinion with the cabinet. The unicameral, or one-house, assembly is called the Majlis al-Umma. Its fifty seats are held by members who are directly elected from five districts by a simple majority vote. In addition, fifteen cabinet ministers, who are appointed by the prime minister, function as part of the assembly. Members serve four-year terms. Political parties

A bird's-eye view of Kuwait's National Assembly in session.

have not been legalized in Kuwait, although National Assembly members have formed opposing groups with certain interests. The next elections are scheduled for 2020.

The first National Assembly, formed after independence, frequently criticized the cabinet ministers and government policies, setting a precedent for future assemblies. As the number of disagreements grew, the emir dissolved the assembly in 1976. He was particularly concerned with the ties that seemed to be developing between the Kuwaiti opposition and groups in the wider Arab world, especially considering the large number of politically active, highly educated Palestinians who were living in Kuwait.

Kuwait's neighbor, Saudi Arabia, had never approved of the democratic experiment in Kuwait and encouraged the emir to be wary of possible challenges to his rule. The emir claimed that the members of the National Assembly had spent so much time arguing over issues that budgets and new laws were delayed. Certainly the members had made many enemies from their campaigns against corruption and price controls, campaigns that were popular with the people. When the assembly was dissolved, press controls were also introduced.

To the surprise of many, the emir kept his promise to restore the National Assembly at a time that he judged right, in 1981. The 1979 Iranian revolution concerned the emir, as it demonstrated the dangers of too little democracy and the inability of a strong government to control a disgruntled population. By encouraging Islamist candidates to stand for election, the emir hoped to include the religious opposition in the government. Excluding them, as Iran had done, could lead to a revolutionary opposition.

THE RIGHT TO VOTE

Kuwait is divided into five electoral regions, each of which elects ten members to the National Assembly. A Council of Ministers is appointed by the prime minister and approved by the emir.

The right to vote was originally restricted to Kuwaiti men. In 1985 only 57,000 Kuwaitis, fewer than 5 percent of the total residential population of 1.5 million, could vote.

In 2005, however, the National Assembly passed legislation allowing women to vote and run for parliament for the first time in Kuwait's history. In addition, all Kuwaiti citizens over twenty-one years of age can now vote, except for active members of the armed forces and the police, who are also barred from serving in the National Assembly. In the 2016 elections, voter turnout was about 70 percent of the 483,000 registered voters. However, most residents of Kuwait are foreign workers and are not citizens and so do not have the right to vote.

In 2017, however, legislators discussed lowering the voting age to eighteen in order to involve younger people in the election process, and also to bring Kuwaiti practices in line with much of the rest of the world.

ISLAMISTS AND LIBERALS

Liberal political groups in Kuwait hoped that removing Saddam Hussein from power in Iraq in 2003 would strengthen their efforts to modernize the country. However, in subsequent elections, traditionalist and Islamist political groups made steady gains.

Islamists are those who believe that the country should be run as an Islamic state, according to the guidance of the Qur'an and Islamic law. Islamic groupings include the Islamic Salafi Alliance and the Islamic Constitutional Movement (ICM), or Hadas, which is an offshoot of the Muslim Brotherhood. These groups seek the introduction of *sharia*, or Islamic, law and oppose women's suffrage.

By contrast, liberal groups such as the National Democratic Alliance (NDA) believe that Kuwait should abide first and foremost by the laws of its constitution. The NDA campaigned for the political empowerment of women and stresses the importance of uniting Kuwaiti citizens under the umbrella of nationalism rather than dividing them into sects, tribes, and religious

Safaa al-Hashem, the only woman elected to Kuwait's National Assembly, celebrates her victory in 2016.

DIWANIYA: PART OF THE DEMOCRATIC TRADITION

In addition to its elected National Assembly, Kuwait has a traditional institution, the diwaniya (dee-WAHN-ee-yah), which allows Kuwaiti men and, sometimes, women to debate and discuss their opinions and to channel these views to their rulers. When Kuwait was a small city-state, this system ensured that Kuwait was a fairly democratic society where most people could express their views.

Traditionally the diwaniya is a social gathering for men, usually held in a special reception room, also called a diwaniya. These meetings are usually held weekly and are attended, by invitation, by groups of friends and relatives who discuss business and politics over coffee or maybe a meal. They are an occasion for many social and business activities and are also a way of establishing contact with people who can carry participants' concerns and opinions to the ears of the cabinet members, or even to the emir himself.

An example of the efficient but complex working of the diwaniya network might be that of a Kuwaiti boss who finds that his construction business is badly affected by a shortage of Asian workers because of government restrictions on the numbers admitted into Kuwait. He expresses his problems at a family diwaniya. His cousin, who works in the Ministry of Defense, agrees with him. At a diwaniya of army officers and their friends, which he regularly attends, he raises this concern. A fellow guest, who is the husband of the sister of a cabinet minister, then agrees to raise the matter at his family diwaniya. Thus the matter is brought to the attention of a cabinet minister, who might then discuss it with his colleagues. If several of them have also heard of this problem, they will formulate a policy to deal with it.

Most people attend several diwaniyas, meeting different groups of people. In this way common concerns will be discussed and conveyed to the highest diwaniyas. When the National Assembly was closed, the emir encouraged the diwaniya network as an alternative to elected assemblies. The network fueled the pro-democracy movement in Kuwait and was instrumental in the resistance to the Iraqi occupation.

The diwaniya system works well for male Kuwaiti citizens who are admitted to this network. Women have their own more informal visiting networks. They may also express some opinions through their male relatives, who might raise their concerns in male diwaniyas. Non-Kuwaitis may have their own networks, but these are unlikely to overlap with those of Kuwaitis.

groupings. Many young Kuwaitis support the NDA. Two Shiite groups, the National Islamic Alliance and the Justice and Peace Alliance, represent Kuwait's substantial Shiite community.

THE BUREAUCRACY

The Kuwaiti bureaucracy, which expanded rapidly after the discovery of oil, is one of the largest in the world for a country its size. Kuwait did not have an extensive administration under the British, and oil exploitation makes few bureaucratic demands. The need to spend the oil revenues was the real impetus to expanding this bureaucracy. The system provided pleasant employment for Kuwaitis, who were no longer required in the traditional industries that were displaced by oil wealth.

As there have never been enough educated Kuwaitis to run this giant organization, many Arabs from other countries, in particular Palestinians, were employed in managerial positions, overseen by Kuwaiti managers or ministers. By 1989 only 44 percent of civil servants were Kuwaiti. At the

The National Assembly building in Kuwait City

A Boeing AH-64 Apache helicopter of the Kuwait Air Force participates in military exercises in 2017.

senior-staff level the percentage of Kuwaitis was higher, at 66 percent, after efforts were made to increase the proportion. This was an overrepresentation of Kuwaitis in the civil service, as only 28 percent of the population were Kuwaiti citizens at that time.

According to recent statistics, the Kuwaiti government employs 345,100 Kuwaitis in the public sector, representing 76.8 per cent of the total Kuwaiti labor force. Despite a vigorous effort by the government to make the private sector more attractive to Kuwaiti nationals, foreigners continue to dominate them.

THE MILITARY

Kuwait has always depended on diplomacy to solve problems with its neighbors. The army was intended merely to delay an aggressor while the government rallied diplomatic support. In 1978 Kuwait was the first Gulf state to introduce national conscription and compulsory high school military training. All Kuwaiti men, including members of the al-Sabah family, between the ages of eighteen and thirty had to serve in the army. Previously the army had relied on Bedouin, many of whom were not citizens, assisted by expatriate advisers.

In 1980 the Iran-Iraq War led to a call-up of Kuwaiti men up to the age of fifty. Despite attempts to make army life more attractive, Kuwaitis were reluctant to serve. On the eve of the Iraqi invasion, the army was only 20,000 strong, mostly non-Kuwaitis, and up to 60 percent of them were on summer leave.

Since the war, Kuwait has modernized and increased the size of its armed forces, mainly with the help of the US military. The government has also sought to improve defense arrangements with other Arab states. Today Kuwait's all-volunteer armed forces are approximately 50,000 strong and maintain more than three hundred main battle tanks to deter invasion from aggressive neighbors. A separately organized national guard maintains security within the country, while police forces are under civil control. Women have been able to serve in the police forces since 1999.

INTERNET LINKS

https://www.al-monitor.com/pulse/politics/2012/10/who-are -kuwaits-opposition.html
This article explains the various political groups in Kuwait.

http://www.bbc.com/news/world-middle-east-14646835
The BBC provides information about the ruling emir.

https://www.constituteproject.org/constitution/Kuwait_1992 .pdf?lang=en
This is a pdf of an English-language translation of the Kuwaiti constitution.

https://www.e.gov.kw/sites/kgoEnglish
This is the homepage for the official site of the Kuwaiti government.

https://freedomhouse.org/report/freedom-world/2017/kuwait
This organization rates and provides a summary of Kuwaiti freedoms.

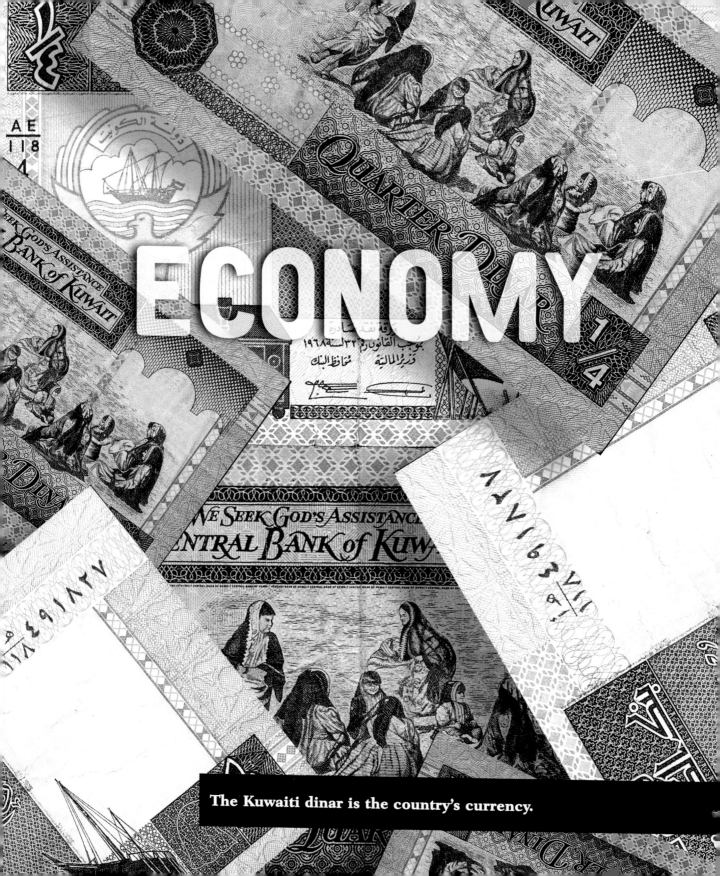

ECONOMY

The Kuwaiti dinar is the country's currency.

4

THE ECONOMY OF KUWAIT CAN BE summed up in one word—oil. Petroleum accounts for more than half of the country's economic production, 92 percent of its export revenues, and 90 percent of the government's income. According to the constitution, all natural resources in the country are state property. Therefore, income from the export of oil is paid directly to the government, which then has to manage that revenue within the domestic economy.

Kuwait is much like its Gulf neighbors in these respects. The economies of the Gulf region are distinct from those of both poorer countries and industrialized countries with which they share a similar or higher standard of living. A per capita income of $69,700 conceals serious inequalities between Kuwaitis and expatriates (persons from other countries living in Kuwait), both in income and in the form of welfare benefits given to all Kuwaitis. In 2017, expats accounted for some 60 percent of the 2.695 million labor force.

Kuwait has few natural resources other than oil. In 2017 Kuwait was estimated to have 101.5 billion barrels, or 8 percent of the world's oil reserves. It was the ninth-largest producer of oil in the world.

TOO RICH, TOO FAST?

Kuwait is the second-richest country in the Arab world, after Qatar. In fact, in some rankings—depending on the methodology—it's the second-richest country in the *entire* world.

Like its neighbors in the Gulf, the country's wealth comes from its oil, and it has been unable to determine how best to spend its oil income. It has spent a good deal of its revenues quite successfully on infrastructure and on health, education, and other services. To be used effectively, imported goods and services require a skilled local labor force, able management, and a strong commercial structure.

Kuwait's excess of foreign exchange has resulted in the development of a "slave" economy, in which many goods and services, together with the labor to run them, are imported. Kuwait depends heavily on foreign laborers who often work in poor conditions. Although they are paid poorly—and often treated poorly as well—they often choose to work in Kuwait because conditions in their home countries are even worse.

Meanwhile Kuwaitis live like masters without serious productive employment. In 2017, non-Kuwaitis represented almost 70 percent of the total population and about 60 percent of the labor force of 2.695 million workers.

Per capita income represented by the value of oil exports divided by the number of citizens is extremely high. Generally a low-quality labor force that demands high income, as is the case among Kuwaiti citizens, is a poor basis for establishing competitive agriculture or industry. In short, Kuwaitis will not work for less money than they can receive from the government simply by being citizens. Producing things in Kuwait would be expensive, as the wages for Kuwaitis would be too high. Apart from very expensive items such as jewelry or bulky items such as furniture, it is cheaper to import most goods from countries where the wages are lower.

WHAT IF THE OIL RUNS OUT?

Oil is a limited product, as is the gas that accompanies it. Kuwait has an estimated 101.5 billion barrels of oil left, which at the current rates of

DUTCH DISEASE

Most oil economies in the Gulf tend to suffer from an economic condition called Dutch disease. This occurs when one sector of an economy (usually a newly discovered natural resource) booms quickly at the expense of other sectors. In the Gulf states, that sector is the oil industry. Other sectors (such as manufacturing or agriculture) are undermined by the easy living gained from oil exports. The term stems from the problems faced by the Dutch economy when natural gas was discovered and exploited by the Netherlands in the 1960s for the first time. Welfare provisions grew, and government employment expanded unnecessarily as the state controlled the oil income. Establishing alternative ways of earning money was neglected.

extraction will last for more than one hundred years. Only Saudi Arabia and possibly Iraq have greater reserves. Nevertheless the Kuwaiti government has long been aware that future generations of Kuwaitis will not be able to rely on a massive oil income. With this in mind the government embarked on an ambitious policy to protect Kuwait's future by creating a government-run investment body (sovereign wealth fund) called the Kuwait Investment Authority (KIA).

Kuwait decided in the mid-1970s not to attempt to diversify its economy but to concentrate instead on refining and exploration techniques. Oil production was kept low to maintain output, and financial resources were invested abroad for future generations. Only 10 percent of Kuwaiti oil is used within the country, as it is considered too valuable to burn. The laws to protect Kuwait's future generations oblige the government to invest 15 percent of oil revenues through the Future Generation Fund (FGF) in long-term investments, mostly abroad. These investments account for half of the total revenue generated in Kuwait. Nearly 70 percent of this income is not spent but reinvested.

The KIA is thought to have about $592 billion in assets, making it one of the largest sovereign wealth funds in the world. No assets can be withdrawn from the FGF unless sanctioned by law. The government owns many commercial ventures around the world and has substantial holdings in most

BLACK GOLD

Oil was discovered in Kuwait in 1938, but the first exports were not made until 1946. Kuwait benefited from the closure of the Iranian oil fields during a period of political

unrest in 1951, as well as from the discovery of new oil fields at Mina al-Ahmadi. By 1953 Kuwait had the largest output of all the countries in the Gulf area. Its production was not overtaken by any of its neighbors until 1965.

Oil is very easy to extract in Kuwait— it's under such natural pressure that it comes spouting out of the ground. Most oil wells in Kuwait are sited on a slight incline so that the oil can easily be moved by gravity through pipes to the coast, where it is refined.

Kuwait has followed a policy of extracting, refining, and retailing oil. This means it is able to sell higher-priced products rather than lower-priced crude oil. By the mid-1980s, 80 percent of Kuwait's crude oil was refined locally, and 250,000 barrels per day of refined oil were sold as gasoline from 4,400 Kuwaiti-owned gas stations in Europe, under the Q8 logo. Today there remain hundreds of Q8 gas stations in Belgium, the Netherlands, and Sweden. Kuwait has its own tanker fleet to export the oil. It is also involved in the extraction and refining of oil in other countries and has a well-developed petrochemical industry that uses oil by-products.

of the New York Stock Exchange's leading corporations, as well as in most European countries and in the emerging markets of East Asia.

Thanks to these extensive investments outside the Middle East, the Kuwaiti government was able to function, without resorting to borrowing, during the Iraqi invasion and the time that it took to restart oil production.

A RENTIER ECONOMY

Economists and political scientists call oil economies like Kuwait's rentier economies. In a rentier economy, the state derives all or a substantial portion of its national revenues from the rent of its natural resources to external clients. (In this case, the word *rent* is used as an economic term, meaning any excess payment required by the owner of the resources to allow business to take place.) In such an economy, the source of income, or rent, is externally generated, involves little contact with the local economy, goes directly to the state, and is very large.

In Kuwait, revenues have historically come from foreign oil companies. The oil industry creates few related industries, generates money rather than jobs, and is capital intensive—it uses money rather than people.

Revenues from oil go to the state, unlike in most other countries where income from foreign trade goes to the companies that make and export goods. Before oil was discovered, the sheikhs collected taxes on pearling and trading boats.

The state owns the land where oil is found or the rights to exploit it, so it also owns the income from oil. Kuwait's oil revenues account for more than half of its gross domestic product (GDP), 92 percent of its export revenues, and 90 percent of its government income.

THE EFFECTS OF OIL DEPENDENCY

Kuwait's rentier economy has affected the nature of the Kuwaiti state. A rentier state has a different function from that of other states. In most countries, the government collects taxes to pay for the workings of the government, which provides certain goods and services that benefit the entire population.

In Kuwait there are few taxes, and the government simply distributes oil revenues through direct transfers, social services, and state jobs. The country has no Internal Revenue Service, but it does have ministries for health, social affairs, and education. It also has a large ministry for oil. The Kuwaiti government can distribute revenue, but it cannot redistribute wealth—that

CITY OF SILK

To augment Kuwait's dependence on oil, the government is investing in the construction of a new commercial center that will function as a regional trading and tourism hub. The planned $132 billion Madinat al-Hareer (City of Silk) is the largest real estate development project in the Middle East.

The development, to be built in Subiya, in the remote north of the country, will include the Burj Mubarak al-Kabir, the world's tallest structure; a desert nature reserve of 0.8 square miles (2 square km); a large business center; environmental areas; sports areas; and tourist attractions, such as hotels, spas, and public gardens.

Officials walk the construction site of the Jaber Causeway in 2017.

The project was approved in 2008 by the Kuwaiti government, but it then sat on hold until 2014 when the final master plan was approved. Construction of the 22.4-mile (36 km)-long Jaber Causeway and bridge from Kuwait City to the Subiya site has begun and is expected to open in 2018. The new complex itself will probably take up to twenty-five years to complete.

is, it can give to the poor, but it cannot take from the rich. This means that the state has limited economic policy tools and little flexibility.

As in other rentier economies, oil weakened certain old classes in Kuwait, such as the merchants, because the state no longer needed their taxes, and Kuwaitis no longer depended on them for employment. If oil wealth destroyed certain social groups, it also created a new one: a huge class of civil servants and bureaucrats who depend on the state for their existence.

In Kuwait the state was initially stable as it created a new social structure. But with no taxation, the government does not need to consider the wishes of the people, because their money is not being spent. Being wealthy also means the government is able to buy the support of some people. Kuwaitis have recently shown, however, that they are no longer content simply being wealthy but want more say in shaping the country.

Another drawback of a rentier economy is that it is dependent on the outside world. Kuwait relies on other countries for food, water, and most of its consumer goods and raw materials. It must rely on foreign markets and the price they are prepared to pay for oil; it also relies on foreign labor and imported goods.

KUWAITIZATION

The Kuwaiti government has come around to the idea that Kuwaitis should learn to do the work their country needs, and stop outsourcing work to expats from other countries. This workforce nationalization initiative takes several forms. On the one hand, the government is looking to fill all civil service jobs with Kuwaitis only. Some 1 million expatriates are to be replaced by local Kuwaiti nationals such that the government is 100 percent "Kuwaitized" by 2022. (Some critics and skeptics question whether enough Kuwaitis have sufficient expertise in certain specialized fields.)

The other part of the plan involves trying to get more private companies in Kuwait to hire Kuwaitis, and persuading more Kuwaitis to consider working for private companies. A 2016 report found that more than half of Kuwaitis are unwilling to join the private sector. The benefits of working in the public sector greatly outweigh those provided by the private sector— higher salaries, better benefits and perks, fewer working hours, and more job security. Kuwaitis are rarely fired from public sector jobs regardless of their productivity. Rather than work for a private company, many Kuwaitis prefer to stay unemployed and wait for a job to open up in the public sector.

The reasoning behind the Kuwaitization push is unclear. Expats are blamed for a slew of problems, from drug addiction to traffic congestion and environmental pollution. Indeed, some politicians point to expat-caused

DOMESTIC WORKERS

As Kuwaitization progresses in skilled labor fields, it's unlikely the Kuwaitis themselves are keen to fill the more lowly positions. Among the many foreign workers in Kuwait are hundreds of thousands of domestic servants, mainly from India, Sri Lanka, and the Philippines. Precise figures of the number of domestic workers are hard to confirm, but some estimates suggest there is one domestic servant for every two Kuwaitis.

Most are young Asian women employed by families to cook meals, clean the home, and look after the children. In the past the working conditions and salary levels were not regulated by the government. Some domestic servants complained of abuse by employers, which included not being allowed a day off, working up to fifteen hours a day, and not being paid on time. Some complained of enslavement—being beaten, locked in their rooms, and refused permission to go outside the home. A standardized contract for foreign domestic workers introduced in October 2006 led to few improvements, and abuses still persist.

The situation came to a head in 2018 when the body of a Filipino domestic worker was found in a freezer in an apartment in Kuwait. Her body indicated she had been terribly beaten and tortured. In response to that murder, and many other claims of abuse, the Philippines government barred its citizens from traveling to Kuwait for employment.

traffic accidents claiming the lives of Kuwaiti children, and medical errors by expat doctors causing the deaths of Kuwaiti citizens. Outsiders are also accused of using up the country's social services. In 2018, Safaa al-Hashem, Kuwait's only female member of parliament, said, "Expats are opportunistic bacteria."

To achieve the goal of a nationalized workforce, the government has taken a number of steps including preventing outsiders from obtaining drivers' licenses and barring them from public hospitals. In 2018, Kuwait banned the recruitment of expats under the age of thirty.

ORGANIZATION OF PETROLEUM EXPORTING COUNTRIES

The Organization of Petroleum Exporting Countries (OPEC) was established in 1960 by five oil-producing countries—Iraq, Iran, Venezuela, Saudi Arabia, and Kuwait—as a reaction to the policies of the large international oil companies, which controlled prices and kept most of the profits. At the time, these five countries were producing 85 percent of the world's oil. OPEC aimed to raise international oil prices and increase the share of the profits that the producing states received.

Oil Minister Essam al-Marzouq speaks at an OPEC meeting in Kuwait.

OPEC's membership grew to include fourteen countries, which include most of the Arab Gulf states. Kuwait later also joined the Organization of Arab Petroleum Exporting Countries (OAPEC), which coordinates energy policies among oil-producing Arab nations.

In 1973, OAPEC boycotted Israel and its supporting countries, cut production, and raised oil prices by 70 percent, causing a world oil crisis. For the oil-exporting countries, the embargo was the first experience of leveraging their collective production for political gains.

OPEC and OAPEC have allowed countries such as Kuwait to bargain for favorable oil prices and to agree on production levels to maintain those prices. The Iraqi invasion of Kuwait illustrated that not all of the members agreed on production levels and prices.

INTERNET LINKS

https://www.nordeatrade.com/dk/explore-new-market/kuwait /economical-context

This site provides an overview of Kuwait's economy.

http://www.opec.org/opec_web/en/about_us/165.htm

OPEC's facts and figures about Kuwait are listed on this page.

ENVIRONMENT

Kuwait is a stopover for migratory flamingoes in the colder months.

5

KUWAIT HAS A HARSH, ARID climate, with scarce water resources and poor soil. In such a climate, the main environmental concerns are water shortages, desertification (the transition of fertile land into desert), and the pollution of the marine and coastal environment, especially after damage caused by the Iraqi occupation in 1990—1991.

The government of Kuwait supports a number of organizations in protecting and preserving the local environment. These include the Environment Public Authority (EPA), which was established in October 1996. The EPA is mainly concerned with preserving natural resources, although it also monitors the state and quality of air, water, and soil. Kuwait is a member of the Regional Organization for the Protection of the Marine Environment, which has its headquarters in Kuwait City. Along with other countries in the Gulf, each year on April 24 Kuwait observes Regional Environment Day. Public projects in schools and government departments try to raise awareness of the threats to the local marine and land environments.

WATER RESOURCES

As a small desert country with little rainfall, Kuwait has extremely limited freshwater. In the past, Kuwait spent large sums of money trying to find local underground water, but with little success. Until the 1950s, all drinking water was transported to Kuwait by boat.

However, Kuwait's oil wealth has allowed it to develop some of the world's largest and most modern desalination facilities. Desalination is a method whereby salt water is treated to remove excess salt so that the water can be used for drinking, cleaning, watering crops, and other activities. Desalination is an expensive process and much more costly than taking water from rivers or underground. Desalination plants provide most of the potable water in Kuwait today.

Most of Kuwait's water is desalinated through a method called multistage flash distillation. Seawater is distilled by converting a portion of the water into steam in a series of stages. The steam is then converted back into water that can be used for irrigation, drinking, and cleaning.

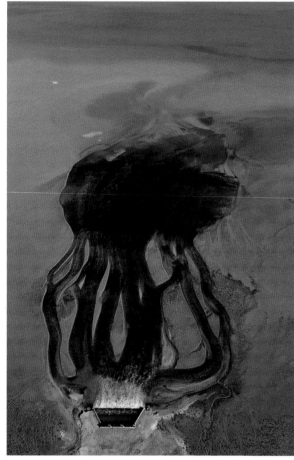

This satellite view shows the waste from a seawater desalination plant in Al-Doha.

DESERTIFICATION

Desertification—the turning of fertile land into desert—is a serious problem in Kuwait. Desertification has been exacerbated by the development of the oil industry, the expansion of cities, water and wind erosion, and the damage caused by the Iraqi occupation and other wars in the Gulf region. Natural vegetation has deteriorated to the point where it covers less than 10 percent of the country and is decreasing at a rate of 110 square miles (285 square km) each year.

Every two years, Yale University, in collaboration with Earth Institute and the World Economic Forum, releases a report called the Environmental Performance Index (EPI) which ranks the world's countries. In the 2018 EPI, Kuwait ranked number 61 out of 180 nations; fifth in the Middle East/North Africa region. (For comparison, Switzerland ranked first, Burundi ranked last, and the United States ranked 27.) The EPI is an aggregate score based on each country's performance on twenty-four environmental indicators. Some of these include air quality, biodiversity and habitat, forests, climate and energy, water resources, and agriculture.

The EPI reveals a conflict between two dimensions of a nation's development—its environmental health, which tends to rise with economic growth and prosperity; and its ecosystem vitality, which is stressed by industrialization and urbanization. The critical factor in achieving a balance of these oppositional forces depends on the government.

In 2018, Kuwait performed well in biodiversity and habitat, and fairly well on water resources and wastewater treatment. But it fell down in the climate and energy category for its carbon dioxide emissions, where it ranked a very dismal 172 out of 175. Energy and transport systems release this and other heat-trapping gasses into the atmosphere. Kuwait's heavy density of cars contributes to this problem, which in turn causes global warming and climate change.

Kuwait also did poorly on exposure to lead and heavy metals. Lead, arsenic, mercury, and cadmium are hazardous to human health, particularly in children and pregnant women. Sources of these so-called heavy metals vary, but human exposure is largely attributed to mining and industrial operations, including metal refineries, power plants, electronics manufacturing—and the most likely culprit in Kuwait's case—petrochemical production.

The government has made several attempts to combat desertification. It has carried out the mass planting of local flora and other plants that can endure harsh climatic conditions. The government has also sponsored studies of the soil and climate to determine which plants are best suited to the harsh, dry conditions so that these plants can be nurtured.

The Iraqi occupation forces caused environmental damage on an unprecedented scale. Three days into the war, Iraqi troops opened the valves on the Mina al-Ahmadi Sea Island Terminal, releasing millions of gallons of oil into the waters of the Gulf. Estimates vary, but it is thought that 6–8 million barrels of crude oil were spilled into the marine environment. The resulting oil slick was more than 100 miles (161 km) long and 40 miles (64 km) wide. At least 286 miles (460 km) of coastline, most of it in Saudi Arabia and Bahrain, were affected, devastating coastal wildlife and destroying large areas of mangroves. Migratory birds, cormorants, dolphins, and turtles were all heavily affected. The corals that form the base of the ecosystem of the warm shallow Gulf were poisoned by oil. With the corals damaged or destroyed, many of the creatures that lived off them also died. Many birds

died because they drank from the oil spills thinking they were water. The slick was fought by crews from international oil companies, and eventually around a million barrels of crude oil were recovered from the slick.

The retreating Iraqi army set fire to between six hundred to seven hundred oil wells—almost two-thirds of the wells in the country—and the fires burned for eight months. With at least 2 million barrels of oil lost each day, this was an environmental disaster of catastrophic proportions. Experts calculated that this waste increased world oil consumption by 5 percent and the worldwide output of carbon dioxide by about 2 percent for as long as it was allowed to continue. After months of intensive work, twenty-eight international firefighting crews put out the fires, at a cost of $1.5 billion to Kuwait.

The burning of the oil wells dramatically affected air quality, releasing 2 million tons (2.03 million metric tons) of carbon dioxide into the atmosphere and creating a cloud that blocked out the sun for many days. The toxic air caused breathing problems among many Kuwaitis, and people throughout the Gulf region developed asthma. Smoke from

the Kuwait oil fires also dramatically altered weather patterns throughout the Middle East during 1991. Lower atmospheric wind blew the smoke along the eastern half of the Arabian Peninsula, and cities such as Dhahran, Riyadh, and Bahrain experienced days of smoke-covered skies and harmful carbon fallout. The long-term health effects of this extraordinary and deliberate disaster have not been evaluated.

The sabotage of the oil wells also damaged the desert environment. Unlit oil from the wells formed about three oil lakes that contaminated around 40 million tons (40.6 million metric tons) of sand and earth. The oil lakes evaporated to create toxins that poisoned the air and damaged the health of both humans and animals. Intensive cleaning by the Kuwaiti authorities meant much of the oil was cleared by 1995, but the dry climate also partially solidified some of the lakes. Over time the oil has continued to sink into the sand. In recent years, experts have, through various processes of composting and venting (airing), turned the oil lakes into soil of such a good quality that it could be used to create landscape gardens. The creation of the Japanese Garden in al-Ahmadi offers hope that other oil-damaged lands can also be made biologically useful.

AIR POLLUTION

The Kuwaiti national flower is the arfaj.

Along with its Gulf neighbors and the United States, Kuwait is considered among the most carbon-polluting countries in the world, partly because of its oil-producing activities but primarily because of the huge number of vehicles per capita. Low fuel costs and a high level of earnings have created conditions where there are more than a million vehicles on Kuwait's roads—one vehicle for every 2.5 residents—which create 105,169 kilotons (95,408 kt) of carbon emissions each year, or 0.26 percent of the world's total carbon emissions, and one of the highest per capita rates in the world.

PLANT LIFE

Less than 0.3 percent of Kuwait is forested. The little forest that does exist has remained stable in recent years. Kuwait is home to about four hundred species of plants, the most common of which are bright green rimth and red-flowered al-awsaj, both of which are popular grazing plants for camels. During winter there is a remarkable amount of plant life in Kuwait, enough to provide food for local camel herds. Unfortunately overgrazing by goats and sheep is damaging the desert's natural plant life. The arfaj, a bushy desert shrub with small yellow flowers, is the national flower of Kuwait. It is also a main grazing plant for camels and sheep.

ANIMAL LIFE AND ENDANGERED SPECIES

There are twenty-five mammal species native to Kuwait. According to the International Union for Conservation of Nature, none are critically endangered, one is endangered, four are vulnerable, and one is near threatened. Over the past century, the country has seen the extinction of the Arabian wolf, Arabian oryx, striped hyena, jackal, honey badger, gazelles, sand cat, Ruppell's fox, and Cape hare.

One of the hazards for military forces serving in Kuwait (and Iraq) is the existence of several species of venomous snakes. Among the most dangerous is the black desert cobra, or black desert snake, which has extremely toxic venom. However, it is a species very rarely seen by humans. In Bedouin folklore, the snake is said to be so dangerous that if it is killed, its spirit will return to destroy its attacker.

The national animal of Kuwait is the Arabian camel, or dromedary. This animal has provided transportation and food for the people of this desert region since ancient times.

It is estimated that eighteen species of bird breeds are indigenous to Kuwait, the most common of which is the desert lark. Because Kuwait lies at the crossroads of several important migratory routes, the total bird count for the country is around three hundred species. Inland birds of prey such as the kestrel and the short-toed eagle can be seen hunting for big-eared fennecs and the ever-present jerboas. Common lizards include dhoubs (a type of monitor lizard), and dung beetles and scorpions can be seen everywhere. Each April the globally threatened lesser kestrel (Falco naumanni) can be seen passing over Kuwait City.

A lesser krestel finds a snack in the sandy Kuwait soil.

To the north of Kuwait Bay, the cliffs of Jal Az-Zor Ridge are home for many migratory falcons that perch along the ridge in the early morning. The region, which includes a ridge and coastal sand dunes, salt marshes, and mudflats, has been turned into a protected area known as Jal Az-Zor National Park. The migrating black vulture passes through this area in March and October, while the imperial eagle, as well as the lesser kestrel, can be seen in March and October/November.

The reed-lined pools of the Al Jahra wetlands are also a haven for numerous bird species, especially the buzzard, the spotted eagle, the steppe eagle, the imperial eagle, the marsh harrier, the lesser kestrel, and the black vulture.

Pearly goatfish, spiked tripod fish, and silver pomfrets are among the many colorful species of fish caught by fishermen in Kuwait Bay. Crabs and mudskippers are also residents of Kuwait's rich marine environment. All of these fish provide tasty snacks for black-winged stilts, teals, terns, and Socotra cormorants, which also share the coastline. Flamingos are also found in Kuwait Bay.

NATIONAL PARKS

The nature reserve on Bubiyan Island (333 square miles; 863 sq km) is one of Kuwait's few national parks. Bubiyan is linked to the mainland by a 1.5-mile (2.4 km) concrete girder bridge over the Khor al-Sabiya Channel; the bridge is used only by the military. Consisting mostly of marshland and creeks, Bubiyan Island is home to wading birds and numerous coastal marine animals. It was heavily mined during the Gulf War.

In 2003 the Jaber al-Kuwait Marine Life Park was opened by the minister of energy, Sheikh Ahmad al-Fahad al-Sabah, during a special underwater ceremony. Accompanied by a group of divers, the minister laid some stone

The mudflats of Bubiyan Island are far from the bustle of Kuwait City.

blocks designed to encourage the growth of coral reefs. The Jaber al-Kuwait Marine Life Park, like the nineteen other sea reserves already in existence, was set up to encourage marine life back into Kuwaiti waters after the pollution and destruction suffered during the Iraqi occupation of 1990—1991.

In 2004 the Sabah al-Ahmad Wildlife Reserve was opened. The park had been established in the early 1990s as the National Park of Kuwait, near Subayhiyah, in the northeast of the country. Covering 124 square miles (320 square km), the reserve is a sanctuary for flora and fauna and includes a diverse environment encompassing hills, sandy beaches, and muddy coastal waters. The wildlife protected in the reserve includes local rare animals and plants. The Kuwaiti government sees the reserve as an asset for the country's future and encourages young Kuwaitis to volunteer for conservation work within the park.

INTERNET LINKS

http://aqicn.org/map/kuwait
A real-time report of air quality in Kuwait City can be found at this site.

https://epi.envirocenter.yale.edu/epi-country-report/KWT
This is the Kuwait profile page for the EPI.

https://www.nasa.gov/mission_pages/landsat/news/40th-top10 -kuwait.html
This NASA site shows satellite photos of the Kuwait oil fires.

KUWAITIS

Two Kuwaiti girls smile for the camera in Al Ahmadi.

6

KUWAITIS ARE ARABS, AND THEY identify with other Gulf Arab nations. They share cultural traits with Bahrain, Oman, Qatar, the United Arab Emirates, Saudi Arabia, and Iraq. Gulf Arab culture is a mix of Islamic and Arab culture, with African, Indian, and Persian influences.

More than 98 percent of the population in Kuwait is urbanized, and about 83 percent of the total population resides in the capital, Kuwait City.

Kuwaiti school children dress in patriotic colors for National Day on February 25.

Kuwaiti society, like many others, is divided by class, wealth, tribal affiliations, religion, and aspirations. Although the majority of Kuwaitis are descendants of the Bani Utub families who founded Kuwait, some are of other tribal origins or from other Gulf states, or from Iran.

According to the 2017 figures, the population stands at approximately 4,437,590, with immigrants accounting for more than 69.5 percent. The reliance on expatriate workers has led to Kuwaiti citizens becoming a minority in their own country, and this has created serious social problems.

KUWAITIS OUTNUMBERED

Most of the people who live in Kuwait are not Kuwaitis but foreign workers, mostly from other Arab and Asian countries. The presence of so many foreigners in the country has been a source of anxiety for Kuwaitis, who fear that their culture will be overwhelmed. People from more than 120 nationalities live in Kuwait, and are adherents of almost all religions.

Kuwait's population breaks down into broad ethnic groups—Kuwaitis, other Arab peoples, Asians (primarily Bangladeshis, Pakistanis, Indians, Sri Lankans, and Filipinos), and stateless Arabs, or *bidoons* (be-DOONS).

CITIZENS WITHOUT CITIZENSHIP

Bidoons are thought to make up about 10 percent of Kuwait's population. When Kuwait became independent, citizenship became dependent on proven Kuwaiti ancestry, with family residence dating from at least 1920. This was difficult to prove, especially for nomadic tribes, many of whom had not seen the importance of citizenship when they had had no need of the state. First-class citizenship was given to a third of the native population, another third were given partial or second-class citizenship, and the remaining third were considered *bidoons jinsiya* ("without nationality"), or bidoons. Citizens and other inhabitants were clearly separated in all respects, legally, and socially. Government payments were restricted to citizens only, but in many other respects, the bidoons were treated as citizens and hoped to be recognized as such one day.

Historically many Bedouin tribes lived on the outskirts of Kuwait City and in the desert beyond. Often they served as armed retainers to the ruling al-Sabah family. After independence some Bedouin were offered citizenship in return for military service and support in the National Assembly. Some collected passports from more than one Gulf state, but others became stateless, or bidoons. Many of these stateless Bedouin lived in the desert in or near Kuwait but had no documentary proof of their residence.

Today, these stateless people live in the country they consider their homeland, yet they have no rights. They cannot acquire identification papers, without which they then, in turn, cannot obtain birth certificates, marriage certificates, or drivers' licenses. Without documents, children cannot attend school or receive health services.

SOCIAL DIVISIONS

In Kuwait divisions exist between the very rich and the less rich; there are very few poor Kuwaiti citizens. There is a social division between the Bani Utub, the merchant families who are descendants of the founders of Kuwait—who include the ruling family—and the rest of the citizenry. The lowest class are the Bedouin, many of whom are bidoons.

The ruling al-Sabah family became economically superior after the oil boom; as political rulers, they controlled the revenue. All al-Sabah family members receive a monthly check from the civil list. They marry within the family and hold key positions in the government, as well as in most business, educational, and other ventures. In many respects they are above the law, as any complaints against them are not dealt with by ordinary courts but by family councils.

The oil boom changed the class structure dramatically. Kuwait's rentier economy makes access to the state, rather than access to private property, the prime determinant of wealth. People from the former artisan and trader classes opted for jobs with the state, taking on new identities as bureaucrats and technocrats.

A Bedouin man smiles in Doha.

Nevertheless the merchant class did not disappear. This was because the merchants had established their own culture and interests, with social institutions such as Diwaniyas (social and political gatherings) and marriages between the families. The government found it cheaper and easier to buy their support than to remove them, so the merchant class remained intact as a group.

RELIGIOUS DIVISIONS

The constitution of Kuwait recognizes religious freedom—to a point. It forbids attempts to convert Muslims to other religions. The small, mostly expatriate Christian and Hindu communities can practice their faiths freely and have their own places of worship. There is also a small Jewish community made up mostly of merchant families.

About 77 percent of the population is Muslim. The majority of Kuwaitis are Sunni Muslims, but a minority are Shiite Muslims. The Shiite community is diverse and consists of Gulf Arabs who emigrated from Bahrain and Saudi Arabia with short stays in Iran, and Persian Shiites whose ancestors spoke Persian and who maintain ties to Iran. As they often marry within their own communities, they each have a distinct identity, although they also have a strong Kuwaiti identity.

The Iranian revolution (1978—1979) encouraged some Shiites to complain of unfair treatment in Kuwait by the Sunni majority. This led to the government introducing more discriminatory measures against them, alienating loyal Shiites. During the Iraqi occupation many Shiites remained in Kuwait, because they felt unwelcome in Saudi Arabia, a conservative Sunni society. Shiites are regarded with suspicion by the government.

WAYS OF DRESSING

In Kuwait traditional Arab clothes are worn alongside Western-style suits and dresses, casual clothes, Indian saris, and Punjabi suits. Although some Kuwaitis once felt that Western clothes were stylish and better than traditional wear, they now feel proud of their cultural heritage and realize that their clothes are not only attractive but also practical for the local weather and lifestyle.

Although special sections of the souk (market) sell ready-made, traditional clothes, often imported from the Far East, the discerning Kuwaiti will choose the material to have his or her clothes made by a tailor. Many Indian and Pakistani tailors specialize in sewing traditional Kuwaiti clothes, which they custom-make at low prices.

A Kuwaiti man wears a red and white gatra.

MEN'S ATTIRE The traditional clothes still favored by Kuwaiti men are very similar to those of merchants of the nineteenth century. They consist of a *dishdasha*, or long robe, worn over long, white trousers, or *sirwal* (seer-WAHL). A scarf, or *gatra* (GAT-rah), is worn on the head, held in place by a decorative rope, or *agal*. In summer the dishdasha and the gatra are sparkling white, but in winter, black, navy, beige, gray, or even blue woolen dishdashas are worn, and the white gatra may be replaced with a red-and-white checkered one. A loose, long coat called a *bisht* (beesht) may also be worn, usually in sober colors. A fur-lined coat, or *farwah* (fahr-WAH), is also worn in winter by Bedouin, who spend cold nights out in the desert.

Most Kuwaiti men wear traditional clothes all the time, at least while in Kuwait, and all wear casual versions of traditional clothes at home. It is easy to tell the non-Kuwaiti Arabs, such as the Palestinians, as they wear European clothes to work, keeping traditional clothes for the home. Kuwaiti men also carry worry beads, or *masabah* (mas-AB-bah). Rarely is a Kuwaiti man seen without a set of beads, which are rolled, spun around the fingers, or passed from hand to hand.

WOMEN'S ATTIRE Many professional or young women wear Western clothes, but some will also wear a large headscarf, called a *hijab*, to cover their hair and neck. Other women wear a black *abaya*, a sort of cloak that covers the body and clothes in loose folds. Most Bedouin and older women

Some Kuwaiti women wear the traditional burka, as seen here, which covers all but the eyes.

cover their faces with a black cloth, or *bushiya* (boosh-ee-YAH), or wear a *burka*, which covers both the face and the body.

The most common form of traditional woman's dress is the *thob* (thohb), a long, loose dress. These can be made in any color or fabric and are often lavishly embroidered with jewels, sequins, and gold thread. They may be made of transparent material and worn over another dress and trousers. Kuwaiti women who wear Western clothes to work or outside the house will almost always change into a *dara'a* (dah-RAH-ah), a simple form of the thob, like a housecoat, once they get home. Many women wear Western-style clothes that are made with floor-length skirts, always with long sleeves and worn with the hijab. They may wear smarter versions of the dara'a to work or outside the house.

Kuwaiti women take great care with their appearance and tend to wear elaborate makeup, jewelry, and hairstyles. Most use black eyeliner for their dark eyes, the way generations of Kuwaiti women have done before them. French perfumes waft through social gatherings, and most women visit beauty parlors and spend hours receiving beauty treatments.

THE POLITICS OF CLOTHING The traditional Islamic way of dressing for women was, until recently, considered a matter of private choice in Kuwait. But lately it has become more of a public issue. The Islamist opposition wants Islamic dress made compulsory, but others want it banned from the university and public offices. During the occupation by Iraq some exiled Kuwaitis were influenced by contact with the conservative Saudi Arabians, while others were influenced by Westerners. Their experiences resulted in various views about women, particularly about their clothes.

Women wearing face coverings have been officially banned from driving for safety reasons, but they can still be seen behind the wheel. Some women feel that the Islamist groups offer the only opposition to the government and show their support by wearing traditional clothes. Some women who were brave enough to wear Western clothes in the past now feel they should wear them with long hemlines, or they now opt for traditional clothes.

CHILDREN'S CLOTHES Many Kuwaiti children are well dressed in expensive foreign clothes. Most wear fashionable Western clothes on a daily basis, and many shops sell imported designer clothes that cost more than they do in London or Paris.

Local tailors do, however, make traditional clothes for children, who often dress just like their parents when they attend social gatherings. The boys will be in dishdashas and the girls will wear thobs and maybe even miniature abayas. All children attending state schools wear uniforms.

In this picture of a Kuwaiti mother and her children, the young boy wears a traditional men's head covering, but the little girl is young enough to appear in public unveiled.

INTERNET LINKS

http://www.aljazeera.com/indepth /inpictures/2013/06/201361417936140789.html
This news site presents a photo-essay about the bidoon people of Kuwait.

http://worldpopulationreview.com/countries/kuwait-population
This site provides an overview of the demographics of Kuwait.

LIFESTYLE

A father and his little son enjoy a walk on a wharf.

7

KUWAIT IS A COUNTRY OF VERY visible wealth and conspicuous consumption. Kuwaitis like to have the newest and best of everything. They also generally have a lot of time on their hands, thanks to their short working hours.

By far, most people live in the coastal cities, where everyone drives, or is driven, in their plush air-conditioned cars between air-conditioned houses, shopping malls, and offices. Kuwait is, on the whole, clean and organized. Few traces of antiquity remain, and these are now carefully preserved.

A mother and daughter check out the latest fashions at the Souq Sharq, a major shopping mall in Kuwait City.

Kuwaiti family law is largely based on Islamic law, which treats men and women quite differently. Women usually need the permission of a male guardian to marry, and a woman's inheritance is half that of a man's.

Parents watch children play at a colorful playground.

The family is the basic social unit. Naturally, this is true in almost every country, but in Kuwait it is even more so. At the highest levels, the government is based on family ties, and throughout all levels of society, Kuwaiti political, business, and social life continues to revolve around the family.

Despite oil wealth, Western influences, the trauma of the Iraqi invasion, and the impact of the US invasion of Iraq, family values remain conservative, based firmly on Islamic principles. A woman's role in the family as wife and mother, for instance, remains central to her identity despite increased education and participation in the labor force.

Although the Kuwaiti government has provided one of the most comprehensive social-welfare programs in the world, Kuwaitis still tend to see the family rather than the state as their main source of support. The importance of the family is enhanced by Kuwait's small size and population, which allows accessibility to political leaders through family networks, by means of the diwaniya meetings.

THE FAMILY

If the family is the most important unit in Kuwait, children are the focus of the family. Kuwaitis love children, and they are included in almost all social gatherings. Even when there are servants to care for them, parents will still be fully involved in their children's lives. Most forms of entertainment are aimed at families, and there are few social activities that are restricted to adults. The concept of boarding or summer school does not exist in Kuwait. As grandparents may well be part of the family unit, children are generally surrounded by devoted relatives. Some Kuwaitis are concerned about the new generation, as children are usually overindulged, and servants are reluctant to discipline them. Nearly all Kuwaiti families have a live-in foreign "maid" who is responsible for most of the housework and some, sometimes much, of the childrearing.

Children tend to be separated by gender early on, and from the time they are old enough to sit still, boys often attend the diwaniyas with their fathers. Girls stay at home or visit with their mothers, although small girls are welcomed into male gatherings, often with great delight. Children live at home until they marry, and possibly even after that, especially if the parents would otherwise be left alone. Unmarried adults almost never live alone, although they may have separate apartments within a family complex.

Generally in Kuwait one's position in the family depends on gender and age. Men and older people have higher status in the family, and their opinions are the most highly respected. Although the government provides free care for the elderly, it is needed only in the rare cases of old people with no family. Older people live in the family as respected guardians of tradition. It would be a social embarrassment to abandon one's parents. Religious and traditional values ensure that the family provides for all its members.

THE SOCIAL ASPECT OF THE DIWANIYA

For the majority of Kuwaiti men, social life revolves around the diwaniya, a weekly meeting, generally of men who are related and their friends. Over

Men gather at a diwanyia to play cards.

coffee they discuss business and politics, arrange introductions, or grant favors. Diwaniyas may be held at any time but tend to be mostly in the afternoon and evening. Tea and other drinks are always served, as well as snacks such as fruits and nuts. A meal may be served, especially late at night, when the guests may bring with them pots of special food. The style of a diwaniya meeting is usually quite traditional. Guests remove their shoes and sit on the floor. If a meal is served it will be spread on a newspaper or a cloth, depending on the degree of formality, and the food eaten from communal dishes. Men may attend several diwaniyas a week, and there may be hundreds of sessions taking place every night in every Kuwaiti suburb. Typically a man will hold a diwaniya on Saturday and Sunday evenings, and his son will host one on Thursday and Friday evenings. The other evenings may be spent at other diwaniyas or with close relatives.

Perhaps more than in other Muslim countries, Kuwaiti women go out after the evening meal to meet in special rooms attached to mosques or to visit each other, often with the children dressed in their best clothes.

KUWAITI WOMEN

Popular conceptions of the role of women in the Arab Gulf states do not necessarily apply in Kuwait. Women are not enslaved in the home, shrouded in black (unless they choose to be), or denied a public role, especially since they gained the right to vote (remarkably, only in 2005) and stand for public office.

Men and women have different identities and interests, however, and men and women are by no means equal. The family is the center of social life, and women's roles within the family are primarily as wives and mothers. The majority of Kuwaiti men and women marry, and usually remarry if they are divorced or widowed. The few unmarried women live with their families.

The government supports equality between the sexes in several areas. Women have ready access to housing, health care, and education. In 1960 the first group of Kuwaiti women was sent to study at Cairo University in Egypt. Soon after the opening of Kuwait University in 1966, women made up the majority of students (more than 60 percent). Today the percentage of Kuwaiti women in higher education continues to outnumber that of men. In fact, this is true in quite a number of Gulf States. However, the overall achievement of women in social, business, and political leadership roles lags far behind these educational achievements.

Shaimaa Othman Al-Najdhi, a senior director at the Ooredoo Kuwait Company, is the first female engineer to work in Kuwait's telecommunications industry.

In 2015, Kuwaiti women outnumbered Kuwaiti men in the country's labor force. (Kuwaitis made up only 20 percent of the total work force.) Of the 342,417 Kuwaitis who had jobs that year, 188,141 were women and 154,276 were men. In this regard, Kuwaiti women have made more progress than women in most other Arab Gulf nations.

Despite that good news, the 2017 World Economic Forum Global Gender Gap Report placed Kuwait near the bottom of the list of nations in this regard, ranking it number 129 out of 144 countries. The annual report assesses countries on gender parity across four thematic indicators—economic participation and opportunity, educational attainment, health and survival, and political empowerment.

Although Kuwait ranked very high in the educational attainment category, as mentioned above, the country fell down in the other categories, particularly the economic and political. The report said, "Kuwait sees notable improvements in gender parity in professional and technical workers as well as healthy life expectancy. However, it also records a decline in wage equality for similar work and women's share of estimated earned income."

About one-third of working women are teachers, while the others work primarily in the social services and clerical positions, although some are

A banquet table is laden with food at a wedding reception.

active in the business world. Most of the working women are foreigners. The reason for the low number of working women lies partly within the society's attitude toward work, for both men and women.

In Kuwait fewer people than in any other country need to work for salary. Some older Kuwaitis object to women working, especially when this means they would have to come in contact with men. As women live with their families, they must respect the decision of the head of the household, who is, of course, male.

Kuwaitis entertain a great deal, have servants to supervise, and have high standards of housework to meet. There are no state nurseries, and in the past foreign nannies were employed. This became a controversial issue, and there was even a campaign against the influence of foreign nannies on children.

Now women have up to two years of maternity leave at half pay. The working day for state employees is short, usually ending at 2 p.m., so working conditions for Kuwaiti women are very favorable, allowing them to be home in time for lunch with their children. In addition, employers are usually understanding about women needing time off to care for sick children. Nevertheless it appears that just as most Kuwaiti men are ambivalent about work, they are even more conflicted about women working. In 2007 the Kuwaiti parliament passed a law banning women from working between 8 p.m. and 7 a.m., to protect public morals.

MARRIAGE

Most Kuwaitis marry, as this is considered the most socially acceptable situation for adults. Men typically marry in their mid-twenties and women in their early twenties. Mothers assume the responsibility of finding marriage

Muslim men may marry Christian and Jewish women, although it is not encouraged, and they do not need permission from their parents to marry. Muslim women can marry only Muslim men, and they usually need permission from their male guardian to wed. A man may have up to four wives at a time, provided he can treat them all equally. Polygamy, however, is relatively rare. Women can be married to only one man at a time. A man can divorce a woman by stating "I divorce you" three times. He must then pay her a sum agreed upon in the marriage contract so that she can live without him. A woman can divorce her husband only if he does not provide for her.

partners for their children. Kuwaitis usually marry partners agreed on by their family, often from the same wider clan group, which means their partner may be a relative. The government pays a grant to every Kuwaiti man intending to marry a Kuwaiti woman; Kuwaiti men marrying foreign women do not receive money.

Once a marriage is likely, the parents will finalize the details. These include an agreed-upon amount of gold jewelry to be given to the woman by the man's family and possibly some money. The cost of the gifts may quite high.

Within a few months of the proposal, or a year at the most, two wedding parties are held—one for the bride's family and one for the groom's. The groom will wear traditional clothes, and the bride will wear a Western-style wedding dress. Dancing (with partners of the same sex) will celebrate the occasion, which will go on for many hours, with soft drinks, tea, and probably a meal. Kuwaiti families spend as much money as possible on weddings, and this is an important source of social prestige. Hundreds or even thousands of guests may be invited. The government gives all new grooms a loan to finance some of the festivities.

BIRTH

The birth of a child is always a source of great delight and celebration, even more so if the child is a boy. The government gives all parents a cash gift

The concept of "face," pertaining to prestige and reputation, exists in Kuwait as it does elsewhere, but there is an intensity about it in Kuwait that is almost inconceivable to a Westerner. A Kuwaiti spends his life building and maintaining face, and the amount of face that he earns is an indication of the degree to which he serves and protects his family's interests.

Children learn about saving face from early childhood. A child is considered to be an adult when he realizes that his own success is directly related to that of his family's. Every adult's status is affected by the behavior of his or her relatives. This sense of maintaining face lies behind most behavior in social and business settings. Although becoming rich can add to this status, visible failure in business loses it, which is why many Kuwaiti men hold on to unsuccessful businesses.

for each baby born, and it continues to pay a monthly allowance until the child marries or gets a job. In modern Kuwait, women usually give birth in a hospital rather than at home as in the past. The baby will often be swaddled or wrapped tightly in cloth and will be named when seven days old. Boys are always circumcised, and this is usually done in the hospital at a very young age.

DIVORCE

In the past, divorce rates were very low in Kuwait, thanks to the support of the extended family and also because most women were financially dependent. There was also great social shame attached to being divorced, and a woman would generally lose her children to the husband's family. The gradual breakdown of the extended family, greater educational and job opportunities for women, and increasing outside influences, especially during the 1990—1991 Gulf War, have contributed to an increase in the divorce rate. In 1972 the divorce rate was 6.5 percent; by 1985 it had increased to 9.4 percent, and by 2005, 36.5 percent.

In 2017, the divorce rate hit a shocking 60 percent. Some social observers speculate the phenomenon was propelled by so-called "interest-driven marriages." A field study conducted by the ministry of justice suggested that the generous financial assistance provided by the state to newly-married couples was a major factor in this trend. Young people seeking ways to make "easy money" would marry to obtain government loans and benefits, and then, once they received them, mutually agree to divorce. No evidence was offered for this assertion, however. The report also mentioned negligence, the inability to shoulder responsibilities, and adultery as the main causes of divorce. In addition, the interference of families in the lives of couples was also indicated as a cause.

DEATH

Following Muslim tradition, Kuwaitis are buried within twenty-four hours of death. The body is washed, wrapped in white cloth, and carried by men to the grave, where it is buried without a coffin, facing Mecca. There are usually no flowers, and the grave is marked simply with a small plinth or paving slab. Male mourners do not shave, and women wear black. A memorial service may be held at a mosque. Guests express their condolences over the next forty days, keeping the bereaved family company.

HEALTH CARE

Kuwait is divided into five health regions, each with a government-run general hospital. There are several specialist hospitals as well. In total fifteen hospitals and more than seventy local clinics serve Kuwait's needs. For citizens, primary health care is provided by the state through a network of polyclinics. Medications prescribed by a doctor are free at hospitals and government pharmacies. Dental care is also free.

Any patient with needs that cannot be met in Kuwait is sent abroad at government expense. This, however, has led to a phenomenon called "medical tourism." Many Kuwaitis have been essentially vacationing in Europe or the United States, sometimes for months, at the government's expense, all the while claiming to have some medical problem. Either because they don't trust Kuwaiti medical care, or simply because they desire a vacation, patients routinely seek help abroad for problems such as back pain or diabetes that could be successfully treated at home. Almost all Kuwaiti cancer patients travel abroad for medical treatment.

In 2014, the government spent about $1.46 billion on funding some eleven thousand medical trips abroad, according to figures from the State Audit Bureau. In 2016, in an effort to rein in out-of-control expenses, the Kuwaiti government announced it was planning to reduce the daily allowances provided for patients and their companions while overseas.

EDUCATION

Until the 1930s, education in Kuwait was entirely private, consisting of religious Qur'anic schools. Since 1965 there has been free public education for citizens from kindergarten to graduate school.

Although preschool is not mandatory, it is provided by the government and about 88 percent of children entering primary school have attended

Children draw pictures with crayons while teachers look on.

some preschool. Kindergarten is available for all four- and five-year-olds, and education is compulsory (and free) for those ages six to fourteen. After kindergarten, boys and girls attend separate schools, although the universities are coeducational. Classes are small, rarely with more than twenty students in a class. The school day starts early, at 7:15 a.m., and finishes at 1 p.m. All schoolchildren

The entranceway to Kuwait University

wear uniforms, and there is no school on Thursday and Friday, the Kuwaiti weekend. There is a three-month holiday in summer and short holidays for major festivals.

The curriculum includes Islamic education, Arabic language, English, science, math, social studies, physical education, fine arts, and music. Intermediate, or middle, school offers the same subjects along with computer studies, and home economics (for girls). Extracurricular activities are not as important to Kuwaiti children as to American children, although the government provides sports clubs and recreation centers.

Kuwait University, which was founded in 1966, has more than 39,000 students, with more than 2,000 doing postgraduate studies. Kuwait University offers seventy-six academic programs through its seventeen colleges on six campuses. The faculty consists of nearly 1,600 professors and associate professors. The university offers degrees in arts, sciences, education, commerce, law, engineering, Islamic studies, medicine, and health sciences. All the science and engineering courses are taught in English, but the arts, humanities, and social sciences courses are in Arabic. Most students who wish to pursue postgraduate studies are sent abroad at government expense. The Gulf University for Science and Technology, the first private university in Kuwait, opened in 2002. The American University of Kuwait opened in 2004.

HOUSE AND HOME

A new home in Kuwait City exhibits the typical gated entrance and humble exterior with small windows.

Traditional Kuwaiti houses, like many others in the Middle East, present a forbidding front to the world. In the old city, rows of blank, plastered walls give no hint of the houses behind the wooden doors that appear at intervals. These carved and decorated teak doors, with carved posts and lintels, are common around the Gulf, but Kuwaiti doors have distinctive carvings of rosettes.

The plain exterior of the houses has both a practical and a social purpose. Because of the hot climate, it is more practical to live in thick-walled rooms, shaded beneath columned arcades around an open courtyard, than in enclosed spaces. Concealing the courtyard, meanwhile, offers privacy to the women; with no windows they can be totally secluded. Humble exteriors also conceal the possible wealth of the family from jealous eyes.

Traditional houses have an outer area, sometimes with a courtyard and sleeping rooms where male guests can be entertained. For the women there is a smaller and separate inner area, ideally with its own entrance. A staircase leads to the roof, where the family sleeps when the weather is hot. Although air-conditioning means that there is no longer any need for cool courtyards or verandas nor any reason to sleep outside, the separation of public and family quarters remains.

As traditional Kuwaiti houses are made largely of mud, repairs are needed every year after the spring rains. But instead of repairs the houses are often rebuilt. After the oil boom many Kuwaitis did not carry out repairs, and houses were demolished or neglected. Modern houses are now preferred.

Although some Kuwaitis and almost all expat workers live in apartment blocks, most Kuwaitis live in the suburbs of the cities in large houses known as villas. These villas can be built in almost any style, including that of a Spanish hacienda or an Alpine chalet. Almost all villas are white or gray and share certain features. They all have rooftop water tanks and a series of television antennas or satellite dishes. The flat roofs are often surrounded by a wall for added privacy. They are usually square, two or three stories, designed in stone or concrete, and decorated with marble facing, decorative windows, and elaborate facades.

Most are surrounded by a high wall with security gates, and many appear quite ordinary on the outside, a continuation of traditional architecture. The windows are usually shuttered against the heat. Inside the high walls, separate buildings may exist for branches of the family or for the servants. The interiors of houses are spacious, with large reception rooms and high ceilings.

The city skyline and residential suburbs of Kuwait City.

INTERNET LINKS

http://www.bbc.com/news/world-middle-east-35881609
This article examines the Kuwaiti practice of "medical tourism."

https://www.e.gov.kw/sites/kgoArabic/Pages/Visitors /AboutKuwait/CultureAndHeritageCustomsAndTraditions.aspx#
In slightly rough translation, this page of the Kuwaiti government explains the country's culture and traditions.

http://reports.weforum.org/global-gender-gap-report-2017 /dataexplorer/#economy=KWT
The 2017 Global Gender Gap report's statistics for Kuwait are found on this page.

RELIGION

The golden dome of a mosque in Kuwait City gleams against the blue sky.

8

SLAM IS THE OFFICIAL STATE RELIGION of Kuwait, but other religious beliefs are tolerated. Although the Kuwaiti constitution protects freedom of religion, that freedom has certain built-in limitations, provided the practice is "in accordance with established customs, and does not conflict with public policy or morals." This umbrella clause covers a broad field of behaviors.

The vast majority of Kuwaiti citizens are Sunni Muslims, which is one of two primary sects within Islam. The two sects often conflict in parts of the Muslim world, but a small minority of Shia, or Shiite, Muslims also live in Kuwait, mostly without discord.

An estimated 17 percent of the people living in the country are Christians, and about 6 percent practice other religions; however, most of these people are immigrants and not Kuwaiti citizens.

To most followers of Islam, their Muslim identity is perhaps even more important than their Kuwaiti or Arab identity. To them, Islam is much more than a set of beliefs. It is a complete guide for living every aspect of life.

Kuwait lies on the Arabian Peninsula, the birthplace of the Prophet Muhammad, the founder of Islam. Islam means "to submit" in Arabic.

One of the requirements, or pillars, of Islam is that Muslims must pray five times a day. Those prayer times are:
· *salatul-ajr* (dawn or sunrise),
· *salatul-zuhr* (midday),
· *salatul-asr* (midafternoon),
· *salat al-maghrib* (sunset), and
· *salat al-isha* (ninety minutes after sunset).

THE FIVE PILLARS OF ISLAM

Five pillars, or requirements, form the basis of Islam: profession of faith, praying five times daily, giving alms, fasting during the month of Ramadan, and making a pilgrimage to Mecca. The five pillars—along with obligations such as being honest, just, and willing to defend Islam; and the prohibitions against eating pork, drinking alcohol, or lending money for interest or gambling—form common bonds among Muslims.

1. Shahada *(sha-ha-DAH)*	*Professing faith in the form of a recitation— "There is no God but Allah, and Muhammad is his prophet."*
2. Salat *(sal-AT)*	*Praying five times a day in the correct manner.*
3. Zakat *(za-KAAT)*	*Giving alms to the needy or to good causes.*
4. Saum *(sowm)*	*Fasting (not even water) between sunrise and sunset for the twenty-eight days of the Islamic month of Ramadan.*
5. Hajj *(haj)*	*Making the pilgrimage to Mecca at least once during one's lifetime.*

A Muslim submits to the will of God, which was revealed through prophets, including those recognized by Judaism and Christianity. For Muslims the last of these prophets was Muhammad, to whom the Qur'an, the word of God, was revealed by the angel Gabriel in the seventh century of the Christian era. The Qur'an is the holy book of Islam.

The prophet Muhammad established Islam when he founded the first Muslim community in Medina, in what is now Saudi Arabia, in 622 CE. The Islamic calendar starts at this point, so like all other Islamic countries, Kuwait operates with two calendars. Although the Prophet died ten years later, his followers established a vast empire until the Middle East, North Africa, and parts of Europe were united in the Muslim faith.

TIME FOR PRAYER

The most important daily aspect of Islam to most Muslims is the second pillar, the requirement to pray five times a day. The prayers, which are said in Arabic, are directed toward Mecca. Before praying Muslims must wash their face, arms, head, and feet in a prescribed manner. They must also be ritually clean, in that they should wash thoroughly after certain activities, such as using the toilet. Women are excused from praying when they are menstruating or have recently given birth.

Although prayers can be performed up to an hour before or after the set times, it is considered best to pray on time. Prayers can be offered almost anywhere, even in the street, but many men, and some women, prefer to pray in a mosque. Prayer times are announced from loudspeakers on the minarets of the many mosques, and most people will stop work to pray. All public places, such as airports or shopping malls, provide a place to pray. In case the direction of Mecca is not indicated, many Kuwaitis carry a small compass. Adult men try to attend the midday prayers at a mosque on Fridays, the Muslim holy day. This is not just a time for prayer but also a social occasion and a chance to attend a lecture by a religious figure.

Muslim men bow during midday Friday prayers at a hospital's mosque in Kuwait City.

THE GLORIOUS QUR'AN

The prophet Muhammad is understood to be the messenger of the Qur'an, not its author. Muslims consider the Qur'an the final word of God, replacing and correcting the Old and New Testaments and any other holy books. During the Prophet's lifetime, the Qur'an was memorized in parts, but after his death it was written down, and it remains unchanged.

A hand-lettered Qur'an and a newer version are displayed at the Grand Mosque in Kuwait City.

It is arranged in 114 *suwar*, or named chapters, divided into 6,236 *ayat*, or verses. It has no clear beginning or end; all the parts are interconnected by rhyme, rhythm, and meaning. Not even a single dot or letter can be changed without altering the entire text. All Muslims study the Qur'an, and children in Kuwaiti schools memorize all or parts of it and study its meaning and interpretation.

Many of the stories from the Old and New Testaments appear in the Qur'an, often in a slightly different form. For example, in the story of Abraham's testing by God, it is his son Ismael, and not Isaac, whom Abraham is ready to sacrifice at God's demand. The only woman's name in the Qur'an is that of Mary (Maryam in Arabic), the mother of Jesus (Esau), who is revered as a prophet, but not as the son of God. These and many other names in the Qur'an are quite familiar to Christians in their anglicized forms.

THE PILGRIMAGE

All Muslims aim to make the pilgrimage, or *hajj*, to Mecca at least once in a lifetime. Kuwaitis are fortunate in that they live so close to Mecca, which is in Saudi Arabia, on the other side of the Arabian Peninsula. Muslims who make the pilgrimage have the honor of adding the title *hajji*, for a man, or *hajjieh*, for a woman, before their names.

The pilgrimage is undertaken at a certain time of the year, and visits outside this period do not count as the real pilgrimage. All business must be set in order before departure, a leftover from when the journey would take months, if not years. Throughout the journey, pilgrims must not use soap or perfume, cut their hair or nails, or damage anything in nature, and men and women must not sleep together. All men wear two white, seamless sheets of cloth, and women keep their faces unveiled.

The rituals of the pilgrimage, which commemorate certain incidents in the life of the Prophet, last nine days, and each year roughly 2 million people

The life of the prophet Muhammad is considered to be a model for all Muslims. Much of what he said and did was recorded by writers, and these traditions, together with the Qur'an, are used by Muslims as a guide to living.

Born in 570 CE, he was a poor orphan who later worked as a trader. When he was twenty-five, he married his employer, a rich widow of forty named Khadijah, who became the first Muslim. After she died, leaving him with a daughter, Fatima, he did not remarry for many years, until his role as a leader of the Muslims led him to do so. He left no adult sons. Many Muslims claim to be descendants of his family. They call themselves sayyids *and are honored by other Muslims.*

Although he became wealthy, the prophet Muhammad led a simple life and was famed for his kindness to his family and friends as well as to anyone who approached him for help. Although Muslims are proud of the way he led his life and of his achievements, they are careful to distinguish this from any notion that they follow him instead of God and Islam.

perform these ritualistic actions. The pilgrimage climaxes with the slaughter of an animal, which is then given to the poor, and the male pilgrims shave their heads. Many Muslims then visit the town of Medina, where the prophet Muhammad is buried.

THE SHIA

The majority of Kuwaitis are Sunni Muslims, but a significant minority are Shia, or Shiites. The division between Sunnis and Shiites appeared soon after the death of the Prophet Muhammad over the question of who should be the leader. The Shiites felt that Ali, the Prophet's son-in-law, and his descendants should be chosen as leaders. The Sunni, on the other hand, do not believe the leadership of the Muslim world should necessarily pass through hereditary succession, but through trusted interpreters of the faith.

The great majority, some 85 percent, of the world's Muslims are Sunni. Sunni and Shiite Muslims both follow the basic five pillars of Islam but differ

There are more than eight hundred mosques in Kuwait City, from simple neighborhood ones to grand buildings that can accommodate many thousands of people. Many mosques were damaged during the Iraqi occupation, but one mosque that has been fully restored and that Kuwaitis are very proud of is al-Masjid al-Kabir, the Grand Mosque.

Construction of this huge building began in 1979 and was completed in 1986. It lays claim to being the world's most innovative mosque. It can accommodate up to five thousand

worshippers in the main hall, with room for another seven thousand in the courtyard. The mosque provides not only a place of worship but also a massive library and reading hall, as well as a conference center and a reception hall for VIPs.

Its architecture uses various traditional Islamic styles, and the building was constructed using modern technology, combining reinforced concrete, natural stone, and decorative marble. Its minaret, the tall slender tower which has a balcony from which a muezzin *calls Muslims to prayer, is the highest in Kuwait, at 243 ft (74 m). The mosque's main hall boasts 144 windows that provide full daytime illumination. The center dome in the main hall is engraved with the 99 names of Allah in intricate Arabic calligraphy. Engraving panels in wooden doors with quotations from the Qur'an in Arabic calligraphy and Islamic design is a Gulf tradition and can be seen in the mosque's 21 teak doors.

on the interpretation of Islamic teachings, tend not to intermarry, and pray in different mosques. The Shiites have an additional calendar of religious festivals; these are related to events in the lives of Ali and other imams (religious leaders).

THE MOSQUE

There are mosques in most public buildings in Kuwait and in places such as airports, offices, and shopping malls. The most obvious external feature is the minaret, from where the calls for prayer are announced. An indispensable feature is a place where worshipers can wash before praying. A mosque has no furniture, but it is well carpeted so that the worshipers can kneel, sit, and stand in comfort while praying. There is usually a pulpit so that a prayer leader can give a sermon after leading the prayers.

The mosque is clearly oriented in the direction of Mecca. The symbol of Islam, a crescent and star, usually decorates the dome. Mosques are also often used as places for teaching, meeting, and quiet meditation.

In Kuwait women have special rooms or galleries in many mosques so as to ensure that they will not be seen by men. Non-Muslims can visit mosques, as long as they are People of the Book—in other words, Jews and Christians. While in a mosque they must observe the same rules as Muslims. They must remove their shoes to ensure that the floor remains clean and wear clothes that cover their arms and legs. Women must cover their hair, and men are encouraged to wear a hat or other head covering.

INTERNET LINKS

https://www.nytimes.com/2016/01/04/world/middleeast/q-and-a -how-do-sunni-and-shia-islam-differ.html
This article explains the differences between Sunni and Shiite Muslims.

https://www.state.gov/documents/organization/269144.pdf
The US State Department 2016 International Religious Freedom Report on Kuwait is available in pdf form.

LANGUAGE

The death of the late Saudi King Fahd was front page news in Kuwaiti newspapers in 2005.

9

ARABIC IS THE NATIVE LANGUAGE OF about 61 percent of Kuwait's population and the sacred language of all Muslims, who make up 76.7 percent of Kuwait's population. It is the official language of Kuwait, and all government documents and notices are in Modern Standard Arabic.

English, particularly American English, is the second language for most educated Kuwaitis. It is important in business circles, but getting around with just English could be difficult, although street signs and many shop signs are in both English and Arabic.

Many other languages are spoken in Kuwait, reflecting the diverse origins of the many immigrants in the country. In particular Farsi (Persian), standard Hindi, and Punjabi are widely heard in the streets and souks, or markets.

Arabic is spoken by more than 292 million people in the world and is the official language of twenty-six countries, as well as one of the six official languages of the United Nations. It is an important link between Kuwaitis and the rest of the Middle East and North Africa.

Three main forms of Arabic exist: classical, the language of the Qur'an; modern standard, which is used for writing in all countries and for communication between Arabs from different regions; and colloquial or spoken Arabic.

Each Arabic region has its own dialect; that of Kuwait is a mixture of Bedouin dialects and the dialect of the Gulf traders. It is liberally mixed with Persian, Indian, Egyptian, and American words, making it

Arabic has ten sounds that do not exist in English, although some of these sounds are used in other languages such as Spanish. However, it also has some sounds that don't exist in any other language, such as ح which is an *h* sound like that of a throaty huff of breath on a window pane to create a fog.

sound different from other Arabic dialects. Its sounds are a little softer and less glottal (the sound that is made in the back of the throat). This dialect is considered by Gulf Arabs to be somewhat new and hip, in keeping with the image of Kuwait as being a very modern country.

ARABIC: THE LANGUAGE OF GOD

Arabic is more than a mother tongue to Kuwaitis. For all Muslims it is the sacred language in which the Qur'an was revealed by God to the prophet Muhammad. Qur'an means "recitation" in Arabic. Many Muslims believe the Qur'an should not be translated into other languages but read only in Arabic, as it is perfect in its original form. A Muslim prays in Arabic, whatever his or her mother tongue, and all Muslims aim to be able to read and recite the Qur'an in Arabic.

Arabic is possibly the main cultural link among the world's 1.8 billion Muslims, of whom only 20 percent are Arabs. Many common Arabic expressions are derived from the Muslim faith and are used throughout the Muslim world. Examples of common expressions include the following:

as-salaamualaykum . . . . . . peace be upon you (used as a greeting)

wa-alaykum salaam . . . . . . and peace be upon you too (the standard reply)

alhamdillallah . . . . thanks be to God (used whenever good news is given)

bismillah . . . . in the name of God (used before eating or undertaking many activities)

insha'allah . . . . God willing (used after every statement concerning the future)

mashallah . . . . blessings of God (used whenever something is positive)

yaallah . . . . with God's help

waallah . . . . by God; truthfully

Many Kuwaitis like to decorate their homes, offices, and cars with these expressions or with verses taken from the Qur'an. These are written in beautifully flowing calligraphy.

Possibly the most commonly used polite expression in Kuwait is *ahlan wa sahlan*, or "at home and at ease," used roughly to mean "welcome." This was originally used by the Bedouin to greet travelers but is now used by hosts, businesspeople, and tradespeople to mean "relax, be comfortable."

LEARNING ARABIC

Arabic is not entirely strange to English speakers, nor to the speakers of many other languages, as many Arabic words are used in other languages. This is partly because of the discoveries made by Islamic scientists and philosophers, who wrote in Arabic; for example, "alcohol" is from *al-kol*, used by the Arab chemists in the Middle Ages. "Algebra" is from *al-jabr*, as Islamic mathematicians invented many mathematical ideas. *El*, a word for "the" in

A little boy reads a colorful children's book at school.

A road sign displays both Arabic and English.

Spanish, comes from when part of Spain was occupied by the Arabs; *al* is Arabic for "the."

Arabic grammar is complex, but it has some similarities with Greek and Latin. All nouns are either male or female, and the form of the noun differs according to whether you are referring to one, two, or more of that item. Thus it can be hard to identify a noun unless you know all three versions, which can be very different from one another.

Arabic script is written from right to left, and the language is entirely phonetic—that is, it is written exactly as it sounds. The writing is always joined fluidly, and there are no capital letters. Each letter has up to three forms, depending on whether it appears at the beginning, in the middle, or at the end of a word. There are, however, fewer letters than in the English alphabet. Not all vowels are written, as there are fewer vowel sounds than in English, but little marks can indicate the vowel sounds for beginners or in foreign words.

The numbers used in English are called Arabic numerals, as they use combinations of nine figures and zero, or decimal figures, an idea that came from the Arabs via India. There are similarities with the Arabic versions, especially in the numbers 0, 1, and 9.

When Arabic words are translated into English, it is often necessary to use more than one letter to indicate the Arabic sound, and it takes practice to learn to pronounce these sounds.

NAMES INDICATE HERITAGE

Kuwaitis' names are clues to their ancestry. Kuwaitis have a profound sense of their heritage, and many can trace their ancestors to the clans who arrived with the Bani Utub. A few can trace their origins to clans that already lived in the area. Some prominent families arrived later from other Gulf states, and those of Persian origin arrived mostly during the late nineteenth and early twentieth centuries. Kuwaiti names tell a great deal about the person. They indicate his or her parentage, clan, or ethnic origin, and so his or her social importance.

The names of a Kuwaiti man or woman will always follow a set order: a given name, the father's name, and then the surname—for example, Mohammed Abdullah al-Shayah is Mohammed, son of Abdullah, of the Shayah family. The name of a grandfather may be inserted after the father's name—for example, Mohammed Abdullah al-Jabir al-Shayah's grandfather's name is Jabir. Generally speaking, the more important the person, the longer the name. The surname is always that of a common ancestor, and all persons with that name will be related, however distantly.

An exception is Kuwaitis of Iranian origin, whose surname may indicate their approximate place of origin. For example, the surname Behbani means the person's ancestors belonged to the village of Behban.

Women also use their family and father's names. They do not change their names when they marry, as they will always belong to the same tribe and father all their lives. Because marriages between cousins are common, many couples do share the same surname, but the father's name will, of course, be different.

FIRST NAMES Almost all Kuwaitis have Arabic first names, often the name of their parents or grandparents, and most names have religious connotations. These include the names of the prophets or saints, such as Mohammad, Yusef (Joseph), and Musa (Moses), and names of devotion to God, such as Abdullah ("slave of God") and Abdul Rahman ("slave of the merciful one"). Other names indicate good qualities, such as Mubarak ("good fortune"), and Salem ("good health").

Great thought is given to choosing names, often with the help of the Qur'an, and they can reflect events at the time of birth or the parents' hopes for their child. Many men's names have a feminine version, usually by adding the female endings eh/yeh—for example, Amir is a male name, while Amireh is the female version.

Women may have names with similar meanings to men's names. They can also be named after female religious figures, such as Maryam (Mary) and Aisha and Khadijah (the wives of the prophet Muhammad). Additionally, many women's names have lovely meanings, such as Jamileh ("beautiful"; the male version is Jamil), Sultana ("queen"), and Yasmina ("jasmine").

NAMES WITHIN THE FAMILY In most respects Kuwaiti names follow the general Arab conventions. It is an essential part of Arabic and Islamic culture to honor one's parents, and no one can change or give up his or her father's name. For this reason adoption is frowned upon, as a child must always use his or her father's name. People may be referred to as son (*ibn*) or daughter (*bint*) of someone when they are introduced for the first time—for example, Mohammed ibn Abdullah.

Another custom within the family and among friends is to refer to people as mother (*umm*) or father (*abu*) of their eldest son. Thus Abdullah and his wife, Khadijah, once their son Mohammed is born, may be thereafter referred to as Abu Mohammed and Umm Mohammed. This indicates the pride that Arabs have in their children, especially the firstborn son. Many husbands and wives refer to each other in this way. Although it is possible to be referred to as the parent of a girl child, this is very unusual and done only if there are no sons in the marriage. The family, and one's place within it, is really the key to people's names in Kuwait.

POLITE RITUALS

Arabic has many expressions that are part of polite formalities. An acquaintance is greeted enthusiastically, and lengthy inquiries will be made after his or her health and that of the family or any mutual friends. This may last for several minutes. A man will not usually refer to another man's wife unless they are related, but he may ask after the family in general.

It is very rude to rush straight to business without the proper formalities. Generally before business of any sort, tea or coffee will be offered. Kuwaitis are very polite and sociable, and this extends to all areas of life, not just social activities.

Kuwaitis are so polite that they rarely use the word "no," so as not to cause disappointment. Things are usually *insha'allah*, or "God willing."

This is part of the general Kuwaiti culture of avoiding unpleasantness. Kuwaitis tend to conceal their anger in public; it would be a serious loss of face for a person to show any lack of personal control. Kuwaitis show their displeasure in subtle ways, by slight gestures or a faint lack of enthusiasm. These are all easily detected by other Kuwaitis.

Kuwaitis are generally very concerned about their honor and social appearance, or face. This means that they behave in a generally dignified manner at all times. Adult men walk with dignity, sit up straight when in company, and pay great attention to their appearance. Kuwaiti men and women do not touch each other in public. It is common, however, to see women showing great affection to each other in public, while men kiss and hug each other in greeting. Men do not kiss women to whom they are not related. Women do not generally shake hands with men.

THE MEDIA

There are six daily newspapers in Arabic and two in English—*The Arab Times* and *The Kuwait Times*. There are also newspapers in standard Hindi and Urdu. More than sesventy magazines are published in Kuwait.

Kuwait has ten satellite television channels, of which four are controlled by the Ministry of Information. State-owned Kuwait Television first offered color broadcasts in 1974 and today operates three television channels. Popular private channels include al-Rai and al-Watan. Most people have satellite dishes and so receive television programs from all over the world. Television channels that show Egyptian films and programs are very popular.

There is one private Arab-language radio station in Kuwait, and it is music based. Radio Kuwait is state-run and broadcasts programs in Arabic and English.

There are more than 3 million Internet users in Kuwait, so many people are able to get international news, entertainment, and information online.

PRESS FREEDOM Kuwait has among the most open media in the Arab world, and Kuwaiti newspapers often criticize government policy. In 2017, the press in Kuwait was ranked "partly free" by Freedom House, which ranks press freedom in countries annually. Reporters Without Borders (RSF) takes a harsher view, as illustrated by the deep decline in its ranking of Kuwait in recent years. In 2009, the organization ranked Kuwait 60th in the world for press freedom—a relatively high score for an Arab country. But by 2017, that score had fallen to 104th, indicating a growing intolerance by the Kuwaiti government for any political criticism. Not only are journalists not allowed to criticize their own government, but they must also not "insult" neighboring countries, as such criticism could harm Kuwait's relations with other countries.

Still, Kuwaiti journalists enjoy much greater freedom to report than most other Arab journalists. Much of the media is state owned, although some private newspapers are run under the supervision of the Ministry of Communications. The state-owned Kuwait News Agency is the largest media house in the country. The Ministry of Information does censor books, films, magazines, and any other imported material that is considered to offend Islamic or Arab sensibilities.

Presses roll at *Al-Qabas*, the Arabic language Kuwaiti daily newspaper.

The law forbids any criticism of Islam, the emir, or the judiciary. In 2010, the Kuwaiti government closed the Kuwait City bureau of Al Jazeera, the Arab news organization, for covering police use of force to disperse an unauthorized demonstration at Soulaibikhat. In 2013, a Kuwaiti court sentenced the online journalist Ayyad al-Harbi to two years in prison for insulting the ruling family on Twitter. A new 2016 cyber-crime law poses a threat to bloggers and online journalists who post any critical content. In January 2018, the Committee to Protect Journalists reported that a Kuwaiti national security court found independent Kuwaiti journalist Abdullah al-Saleh, a YouTube reporter and former columnist for the Kuwaiti newspaper *al-Jareeda*, guilty in absentia of "abusing Saudi Arabia." It sentenced him to five years imprisonment with hard labor. Al-Saleh fled to the United Kingdom to escape punishment.

INTERNET LINKS

http://www.bbc.com/news/world-middle-east-14646837
This country profile includes a quick overview of the media.

https://www.britishcouncil.org/voices-magazine/surprising-facts-about-arabic-language
Some interesting facts about the Arabic language are included in this article.

https://freedomhouse.org/report/freedom-press/2016/kuwait
This is the Freedom House report on press freedom in Kuwait.

https://www.justlanded.com/english/Kuwait/Kuwait-Guide/Language/Language-in-Kuwait
This article gives good insights into the peculiarities of language in Kuwait.

A bright "I Heart Kuwait" sculpture is displayed outside the Al Hamra Tower, the tallest building in Kuwait.

10

I N MOST MUSLIM COUNTRIES, architecture soars as the highest form of art, and this is also true in Kuwait. But fine arts, folk arts, and pop culture also thrive there, perhaps more so than in some other Islamic nations. The government is dedicated to developing all aspects of Kuwaiti arts, and a great deal is invested in rediscovering lost art forms and encouraging new ones.

Nevertheless, Kuwait's religious heritage profoundly influences its artists. In the past, to paint or show human figures was not allowed, as this was against Muslim traditions; however in the twentieth century, some contemporary Kuwaiti artists, such as Mojeb al-Dousari and Abdullah al-Qassar, began to challenge that restriction. As a result, today's Kuwait has a lively and progressive visual arts scene, with artists of all kinds.

BEDOUIN ARTS

Bedouin art is the most prominent expression of Kuwaiti folk art. The best examples are the textiles woven from sheep's wool; these are called *sadu* (sa-DOO). Wool is hand-dyed and spun and then woven into geometric designs on a portable loom. Traditionally Bedouin women

BEDOUIN WEAVING

The traditional Bedouin name for a tent translates to "house of hair," as both the tent and all its contents were woven by women out of camel hair or wool from sheep. The women wove flat rugs and cushion covers, which were stuffed with clothes and other household cloths, to furnish the tent. Large woven cloths were used to cover piles of bedding, which could be used to lean on during the day as well as to divide the tent into rooms. The women also wove saddlebags to hold their possessions between camps, as well as decorative bridles and saddles for the camels. All this was achieved with portable wooden looms and local materials. Tools were made out of gazelle horns; few Bedouin women owned a pair of scissors.

The wool used for weaving was spun and dyed by hand. The women managed to fit these activities in between cooking and chores such as milking, making clothes, and caring for their children. The finished products traditionally belonged to the men, who could sell them or keep them for their own use.

wove black tents of camel hair with decorative sadu side flaps, cushions, and saddlebags for camels.

Now that most Bedouin live in housing settlements, there are few women learning this craft. In 1978, the Al Sadu Society was established to keep this dying art alive. It is now a weaving cooperative run by the weavers and artisans themselves.

Another Bedouin art form is the ardha, a dance in which the agile manipulation of a sword accompanies drums, tambourines, and poetic songs. Folkloric dance troupes are supported by the government and appear regularly on television and at social occasions such as weddings.

JEWELRY

Gold jewelry has long been a vital part of Kuwaiti culture. For the Bedouin, gold and silver are a portable bank balance, and women are given large quantities of jewelry when they marry, just in case they need to support themselves. Jewelry is the most common gift on such special occasions as a wedding, the birth of a child, and a birthday. The designs of gold jewelry are elaborate and include both traditional and modern touches. The latest creations of famous jewelers in Paris are copied immediately in Kuwait, and it would be hard to tell that these are not the originals.

Many Indian craftsmen also work in Kuwait, and a large section of the souk (marketplace) is filled with passageways lined with dazzling gold displays in shop windows. Since the early days of pearling in Kuwait, its jewelers have been skilled at creating jewelry using pearls, as well as imported gemstones.

A wealth of dazzling jewelry is displayed at the Gold Souk in Kuwait City.

CALLIGRAPHY

Calligraphy, the art of beautiful writing, is one of the most-developed art forms throughout the Muslim world. Islam discourages art forms showing humans or even animals. Calligraphy avoids this restriction and serves to glorify God, as verses from the Qur'an are the words usually chosen. The most commonly chosen verse is the Bismillah, which is the opening verse of every chapter of the Qur'an, calling upon God, the most merciful and compassionate.

Islamic calligraphy is a fine art in itself, shown here on canvas.

Calligraphy is used as a decoration for books, manuscripts, buildings, and household items. It is rendered on paper, leather, stone, glass, china, pottery, ivory, and textiles. Calligraphic designs can be woven into carpets and fabric. They can be rendered in various forms and shapes, from animals to stars to flowers. There are several accepted styles of calligraphy, and artists are always working to perfect them as well as to develop new ones.

THE THEATER

Unlike other Gulf nations, Kuwait has a tradition of theater which plays a major role in the country's cultural life. Like folk arts, the theater has received attention from the Kuwaiti government. The Higher Institute for Theatrical Arts trains actors and performers to degree level and encourages awareness and appreciation of theater in Kuwait. The country has four theater companies sponsored by the government.

ARCHITECTURE

Most Kuwaitis probably feel that their greatest contribution to the arts is in the world of modern architecture. Although architectural remnants of old Kuwait remain, and the government is keen on restoring them, Kuwait lacks

A KUWAITI ARTIST

Thuraya al-Baqsami is Kuwait's most outspoken and influential female artist. Born in 1951 in Kuwait City, al-Baqsami began her artistic career at an early age. In 1969 she became a member of the Kuwaiti Art Society and was awarded a bronze medal in 1971 by the Kuwaiti Society of Formative Artists. She received her academic training in Cairo at the College of Fine Arts during the 1970s before moving to study in Moscow in 1981.

Al-Baqsami received the Golden Palm Leaf award from the Gulf Cooperation Council Biennale in Riyadh in 1989 and in Doha in 1992. Her work is held in public and private collections throughout Asia, the Middle East, the United States, and Europe. She also received an award in literature from the Kuwait Foundation for the Advancement of Sciences in 1993 for her collection of short stories, Cellar Candles, *and the State Award for Children's Literature in 1997 for a book of children's stories,* The Recollection of Small Kuwaiti Fatuma.

A peace campaigner, al-Baqsami considers art to be one of the most powerful means of promoting peace. She has also worked hard to promote women's rights in the Arab world through her work.

the older, elaborate architecture found in many other Arab countries. Local architecture consisted of simple mud and stone single-story houses.

From the 1950s, under a series of master plans, most of old Kuwait was demolished, leaving only the gates to the old city walls. A modern city was built, divided into zones for different commercial activities and for different groups of people to settle in, surrounded by a ring of green parks. Kuwait City, as well as the other cities, became a showpiece for outstanding modern architecture, built in tandem with roads and other public utilities. Many tall water towers, which are often distinctively designed and decorated, punctuate the skyline, as do futuristic, commercial tower blocks. The best example of the blending of the modern with the classically Arabian is the National Assembly Building, which is reminiscent of a Bedouin tent.

The skyline of Kuwait City is dominated by the country's most famous landmark, the Kuwait Towers, strategically located at the point where Kuwait juts farthest into the Gulf. The three towers of this 161-foot (49 m) building

The Kuwait National Museum is the most important repository of the artifacts of Kuwaiti historical and cultural life. It includes art galleries and displays of antiquities and handicrafts. All the antiquities from archaeological expeditions are displayed.

Part of the museum complex, the Museum of Islamic Arts, once housed a priceless collection of more than 20,000 items of Islamic art—huge doors, carpets, rare books, manuscripts, china, jewels—covering twelve centuries. Founded in 1983, this collection, called Dar al-Athar al-Islamiyyah (House of Islamic Antiquities), still constitutes one of the most comprehensive collections of Islamic art in the world.

In 1991 all the artifacts were taken or destroyed by the Iraqi invaders, who also demolished the buildings. The museum has since been restored, however, and most of the artifacts have been returned from Iraq (although some pieces had been damaged by rough handling). In 1997 Muhallab II—a replica of the beautiful 1930s trading dhow (sailing ship) that sat in the front yard of the museum before it was burned by Iraqi forces—was constructed on-site.

have a useful function. Two of the blue-green towers are water reservoirs. The largest of the towers rises to a height of 614 feet (187 m) and is home to a revolving restaurant and observation platform.

Opened in 2016, the Sheikh Jaber Al-Ahmad Cultural Center, also known as the Kuwait Opera House, is an architectural wonder. It was designed to resemble jewels, with complex geometric forms reflecting rays of sunlight. Part of the new Kuwait National Cultural District, it houses a theater, performance, and educational spaces as well as a planetarium.

Nearby is the Sheikh Abdullah Al-Salem Cultural Center, with museums of natural history, science and technology, fine arts, Arabic and Islamic sciences, space, and a theater. Along with the Sheikh Jaber Al-Ahmad Cultural Center, its architecture is intended to create a sense of awe and wonder.

Additionally, the Al Salam Palace, which was badly damaged during the 1990s Iraq invasion, is being restored as a heritage museum to tell the story of Kuwait through the lives of its fifteen rulers.

In the city center, Liberation Tower is the second-tallest building in Kuwait, standing 1,220 feet (372 m) high at its pinnacle. Completed in 1993, it was renamed from the Kuwait Telecommunication Tower to mark the liberation from the Iraqi occupation in 1991. Kuwaitis see it as a symbol of the country's renaissance since the liberation.

The Liberation Tower in Kuwait City celebrates the country's freedom from Iraqi occupation.

SAWT, TRADITIONAL KUWAITI MUSIC

Kuwait has a rich musical heritage, but much of this traditional music is performed out of the public eye. Private parties and diwaniyas—men's evening meeting groups—are typically the venues for this music. Certain diwaniyas are dedicated to musical gatherings called samrah. *At such events, the musicians sit at the end of the room, while the visitors sit in two long lines facing each other. Visitors often join in with clapping and dancing and the separation between performers and audience disappears. These are traditionally all-male events.*

One of the popular music genres is sawt, *or sea music. The Kuwaiti poet, composer, singer, and oud player Abdallah al-Faraj (1836–1903) is largely credited with developing this form, which grew out of the musical traditions of Bedouin and fishing communities. It is well known throughout the Arab Gulf region, and musicians from Kuwait have long interacted with artists from United Arab Emirates, Qatar, Bahrain, and southern Iraq, influencing one another, and extending a sense of Arab unity.*

A mirwas is a drum used in sawt music.

Sawt music is played by three musicians, on an oud (a plucked lute), a mirwas *(a hand-held, two-sided drum) and a violin, with a singer. Two men perform a dance called "zaffan."*

http://bazaar.town
The online magazine *Bazaar* focuses on Kuwait's "urban modernist" lifestyle, with coverage of very progressive arts, fashion, dining, and more—in English.

http://bazaar.town/the-sadu-house
A brief article about the Al Sadu House is accompanied by a slide show.

http://www.barjeelartfoundation.org/artist/kuwait
The works of many contemporary Kuwaiti artists can be seen here.

http://english.alarabiya.net/en/life-style/art-and-culture/2017/10/14/Thuraya-Al-Baqsami-Living-through-joy-and-pain-through-art-creativity.html
The Kuwaiti artist Thuraya al-Baqsami and her work is the subject of this article.

https://kuwaitnationalmuseum.weebly.com
This is the site of the Kuwait National Museum.

http://www.middleeasteye.net/in-depth/features/censorship-kuwait-764920799
This article discusses censorship in Kuwaiti filmmaking.

https://www.qdl.qa/en/hidden-treasures-reflections-traditional-music-kuwait
This article about traditional Kuwaiti music features audio filess and videos.

LEISURE

A rainbow-like entrance leads to Aqua Park in Kuwait City.

11

KUWAITIS HAVE LOTS OF LEISURE time. For many in Kuwait, leisure is almost a full-time job—or occupation, in any event. Kuwaitis pay other people to work so they don't have to. This is what happens when a small country becomes as wealthy as this one is.

All major companies, ministries, and enterprises have their own sports clubs, usually for men only, which often own private beaches. Competitions of various sorts are often arranged between clubs.

The sun sets as people enjoy a dip in the sea at the Aqua Park beach.

So, what do Kuwaitis do with all their free time? Actually, most men do some sort of work, mostly for the government, and may have their own business interests as well. In addition, there are religious responsibilities, which include praying five times daily and attending services. Friday is the holy day. Men and women both have family and household responsibilities, and of course, children must attend school.

Most people socialize with their families and their close friends, who are also usually relatives. Social activities are usually segregated according to sex, even at home, though family members can intermingle. The diwaniyas, or regular social meetings, are definitely segregated, and are an essential part of Kuwaiti social, political, and cultural life. Sharing food and refreshments is an integral part of most socializing in Kuwait.

Not surprisingly, a thriving leisure and entertainment industry has emerged. As it does with most other aspects of Kuwaiti life, the government sees to the provision of leisure activities for the people. There are no nightclubs in Kuwait, and the unsupervised mixing of the sexes is frowned upon by conservative Kuwaitis. If young people wish to go out and meet other young people, they do so in American-style coffee shops such as Starbucks or in one of the international hotels.

SPORTS

The government has invested heavily in promoting sports as a healthy pursuit for young people. There are six world-class stadiums in Kuwait. Kuwait's greatest international success has been in soccer, when the national team reached the final qualifying round of the World Cup in 1982, in France. It had previously won the Asian Cup in 1980. Swimming and equestrian competitors have also achieved international success.

There are more cricket teams in Kuwait than all other sporting groups combined. Other popular sports include squash, rugby, baseball, and fishing. Figure skating and ice hockey are popular, especially in summer. There are several air-conditioned indoor ice rinks; the largest can seat 1,600 spectators. Windsurfing, scuba diving, waterskiing, and Jet Ski racing are also popular. Speedboat racing is a modern version of the dhow races that made Kuwait famous in the region.

FALCONRY Some traditional sports grew out of the activities of the desert lifestyle. For example, falconry arose from the necessity to supplement a meager diet of dates, milk, and bread and eventually evolved into a major sport. Hunting parties used to pursue their quarry on horseback, but four-wheel-drive vehicles are now used. Wild female falcons are trapped and trained for the hunting season, which begins in late fall. A trained falcon can catch up to five birds, such as bustards and curlews, in a hunting session. This sport ends at sunset, when the booty is cleaned, roasted over a fire, and eaten in the desert.

A Kuwaiti man takes a photo of himself with a falcon during a training session in Al-Salmi.

CAMEL RACING Camels were important to Bedouin Arabs, as they were the main source of transportation, textiles, meat, and milk. Traditionally the Bedouin would demonstrate the superiority of their camels' bloodlines in a race. Slender, long-legged breeds were bred specially for racing, and there are official racetracks, as well as desert tracks. A camel's training begins at six months, and while a male camel's career will last up to ten years, a female's will go on for more than twenty. Racing camels are fed special foods, such as oats, dates, and cow's milk.

HORSE RACING The Arabian horse is a famed racing breed and one of the most ancient of tamed horses. It has a distinctive appearance, with a short back, a small head with a concave profile, large intelligent eyes, and a tail that it carries high. All thoroughbred horses are descendants of Arabian stallions. The Bedouin people have bred Arabian horses for centuries. They are always prized, and good specimens are traditional gifts between Arab leaders. Both Arabian and thoroughbred racehorses compete in Kuwait.

SHOPPING: A UNIVERSAL PASTIME

Shopping is a national pastime, and almost any item can be purchased in Kuwait, except banned items such as alcohol. Shopping malls such as the Avenues, Souk Sharq, Salhiyah, and al-Mutthana malls in Kuwait City and the Zahra mall in al-Salmiya provide an American-style shopping experience. These complexes sell consumer goods; food is found primarily in neighborhood supermarkets. Kuwaitis tend to go to malls for entertainment, as these have restaurants, cafés, and fountains. Shopping is often a family activity. Entire families will visit malls, perhaps combining a shopping trip with a meal at a restaurant.

The Old Souk in Kuwait City, which is actually not more than eighty years old, offers something closer to the traditional style of shopping. It consists of covered passages and open stalls, divided into sections according to the products sold, such as fish, vegetables, clothing, and household goods. Many stalls sell only one type of item, such as knives or olives. Tailors have shops in the souk where they make clothes.

A family goes shopping at the Al Mubarkia souk in Kuwait City.

HOTELS, PARKS, AND ENTERTAINMENT CENTERS

Much social life takes place in the country's leading hotels, such as the Hyatt, the Meridien, and the Hilton, all of which have sports facilities and restaurants. Many people meet in the coffee bars or visit the exhibitions. Hotels are the most common location for lavish weddings.

Kuwaiti families like to walk or sit in parks, especially after dark, when it is cooler. Starting from the Kuwait Towers and stretching nearly 15 miles (24 km) along the shore of the Gulf is the Waterfront Project. This park combines attractive brick-and-concrete walkways with rest facilities, playgrounds, and food concessions. The waterfront is lit at night, and there are many entertainment facilities for children, including a miniature train ride.

Entertainment City, which is in the middle of the desert near Doha Village, 12 miles (19 km) west of Kuwait City, is a Disneyland-style theme park offering rides, games, and shows with three themes: Arab World, International World, and Future World. Although this multimillion-dollar complex was destroyed by the Iraqis, it was reconstructed after the war. However, the park closed for renovation in 2016 and expects to reopen in 2021.

INTERNET LINKS

https://www.inspirock.com/things-to-do-in-kuwait
This site provides another look at things to do in the country.

https://www.lonelyplanet.com/kuwait/top-things-to-do/a /poi/361089
This travel site highlights the best attractions in Kuwait.

FESTIVALS

Fireworks light the skies for the fiftieth anniversary of Kuwait's constitution in 2012.

12

MOST OF THE SPECIAL DAYS THAT Kuwaitis observe are the Sunni Islamic holy days. Other festivals that are noted are New Year's, National Day, and Liberation Day. Non-Muslim expatriates living in Kuwait are free to celebrate their own festivals, as are the Shiite Muslims, but employers are not required to grant them those days as holidays.

The beginning of Eid Al-Fitr begins with the sighting of the first sliver of a crescent moon following a new moon.

Kuwaiti schoolchildren perform in a concert for National Day.

THE ISLAMIC CALENDAR

Muslim holy days follow the Islamic calendar, which begins counting years from 622 CE, the year the Prophet Muhammad fled from Mecca to Medina. The year 2018, therefore, corresponds to an overlap of the years 1439—1440 AH on the Islamic calendar. The AH means *Anno Hegirae* (Latin for "in the year of the Hegira.") It is used in the same way Christians and Westerners use AD (*Anno Domini*, "in the year of the Lord"), or, as in this book, CE (Common Era).

Unlike the Gregorian, or Western, calendar used internationally—which is solar based—the Islamic calendar is based on the lunar month, which is only twenty-nine or thirty days long. Therefore, the Islamic year is on a cycle of 354 days, not 365 days, in a cycle of twelve Islamic months.

Islamic festivals don't fall on the same dates of the Western calendar each year, but rotate by moving forward about eleven days every year. It takes 32.5 years before a festival once again falls on the same date in the Western calendar. For this reason, Islamic festivals are not associated with any particular time of year, as are Christian festivals, but can fall in any season.

Kuwait, like other Muslim nations, uses the Western calendar for nonreligious dates so as to be in sync with the rest of the world. It observes the Western New Year's holiday as a courtesy to its many foreign residents.

RAMADAN, A WELCOME TEST OF ENDURANCE

The month of Ramadan is the holiest month on the Islamic calendar. It commemorates the first revelation of the Qur'an to the Prophet Muhammad. It is a time for prayer and fasting. In 1991 Ramadan began as Kuwait was liberated from Iraqi forces, and since then it has an even deeper meaning for most Kuwaitis.

Although it is known roughly each year when Ramadan will begin, its exact start occurs as the new moon is sighted and ends with the appearance of the next new moon. This slight uncertainty adds to the excitement for Muslims, who look forward to this special time, despite its hard tests. During the twenty-nine or thirty days of Ramadan, all Muslims must pray on two extra occasions every day, read the Qur'an, be particularly kind and helpful, and try to fast from dawn to sunset. This means not eating or drinking, not even water. It also means not smoking, possibly the hardest part for most Kuwaiti men.

For Muslims, prayer and fasting during Ramadan give a sense of achievement and closeness to the rest of the Muslim world. Children, women who are pregnant or with small babies, the elderly, and the sick are not expected to fast. Those forced to travel are also excused, although they are expected to make up for the days missed on another occasion. Many people feel fasting is good for the health and teaches self-discipline as well as enhances sensitivity to the suffering of the poor.

During the month of Ramadan, the day begins before dawn, often in the middle of the night, when a large meal is eaten before sunrise to prepare for the fast ahead. Restaurants are closed, except those that serve only non-Muslims and travelers, such as the airport coffee shops.

The crescent moon signals the start of the holy month of Ramadan.

If the month falls in winter, it is a great relief, as the day is short and the feeling of thirst is not so acute. When the month occurs in the scorchingly hot summer, however, the fast is harder to endure. Many Kuwaitis sleep a great deal during the day at this time, if they can.

After sunset, it is traditional to break the fast with water and a few dates, the sort of food that the Prophet Muhammad would have eaten, rather than eating a big meal immediately. Many people gather in mosques, where dates are served after the sunset prayers, followed by a meal for those who wish to stay.

After prayers, the family gathers again and breaks the fast together. Many traditional dishes are served for this meal, which can last until late in the night. The evenings are occasions for much merriment, followed by visits to relatives and friends, or trips to shops, restaurants, and parks, which stay open late during the month. The whole family often stays awake all night, only going to bed after eating the early breakfast. No wonder children look forward to the fasting month.

There is an additional treat for children in Kuwait during Ramadan—the celebration of Gargee'an (or Qarqe'an). On the thirteenth night of the fast, children visit from house to house, singing to the youngest member of each household and collecting gifts and sweets.

THE EIDS

There are two major Islamic holidays in Kuwait and both are called *Eid* (EED), which means "feast" or "festival."

Kuwaiti children buy fireworks in Kuwait City in preparation for Eid al-Fitr, which marks the end of the Muslim fasting month of Ramadan.

EID AL-FITR (EED AHL-FITT-ER) "The Feast of Breaking the Fast" occurs on the first day of the month of Shawwal, immediately after Ramadan, the fasting month. Eid al-Fitr begins with the men going to the mosque for the morning prayer. This is followed, according to the teachings of the Prophet, by a visit to the cemetery.

Once these solemn religious duties are done, Eid al-Fitr becomes a happy occasion celebrating the end of Ramadan, the fasting month. People dress in their best clothes and wish one another a "Happy Eid." Gifts and money are given to children and to newly married daughters. More significant is the joyous return for all to a normal life.

EID AL-ADHA (EED AHL-AHD-HA) "The Festival of the Sacrifice" commemorates the willingness of Ibrahim (known to Christians and Jews as Abraham) to sacrifice his son to show submission to Allah's command. As Ibrahim prepared to kill his son, God stopped him and gave him a sheep to sacrifice instead.

Although Muslims observe this four-day holiday all around the world, its most sacred observance is in Mina, a small village four miles (6.4 km) east of Mecca, in Saudi Arabia. There, hundreds of thousands of Muslims take part in the activities of the hajj, the sacred annual pilgrimage to Mecca and other sacred sites nearby.

The teachings of Muhammad decree that heads of families who are able to do so must purchase a sheep for sacrifice. The meat of the slaughtered animal is shared with the poor. The person making the sacrifice symbolically affirms that he is willing to give up, for the sake of Allah, that which is dearest to him. It is a sacred gesture of thanksgiving and a measure of charity.

PATRIOTIC HOLIDAYS

Two days mark important events in the history of Kuwait, and both are commemorated according the Western calendar.

National Day, February 25, marks the day that Sheikh Abdullah Al-Salem Sabah ascended to the throne in 1950.

Liberation Day, February 26, celebrates the reestablishment of Kuwait's freedom after the Iraqi invasion and subsequent Gulf War in 1991. One of Kuwait's few patriotic holidays, Liberation Day is a time for Kuwaitis to remember the great sacrifices made in gaining liberation from the Iraqi occupation.

INTERNET LINK

https://www.officeholidays.com/countries/kuwait/index.php
This site provides the most up-to-date calendar for public holidays in Kuwait, with links to explanations.

FOOD

A platter of succulent dates, a favorite fruit throughout the Mideast.

13

THE FLAVORS OF KUWAIT BRING together the cuisines of Arabian, Persian, Indian, and Mediterranean cultures. Spices such as cardamom, saffron, and cinnamon infuse many of the meat and rice dishes as well as the sweets. Dates are perhaps the most beloved fruit, as is true throughout the Middle East. In this dry country, fresh produce must be imported, and isn't a basis for the traditional cuisine.

The time-honored foods in Kuwait are those of the desert Bedouin, supplemented by a variety of fish from the Gulf. Trading, and later, oil wealth enabled Kuwaitis to develop a varied and sophisticated cuisine. Kuwaiti cuisine reflects the long history of trading contacts with other countries and consists of a mixture of Arab, Turkish, Iranian, and Indian food. There is a strong reliance on fish, rice, bread, and fruit. As there are many foreigners living in the country, most Kuwaitis are familiar with a great variety of foods. Restaurants offer a varied fare, but as all food must be *halal*, or deemed suitable by Islamic law, no pork or alcohol is served.

Kuwaiti meals will usually be accompanied by bowls of tomato and garlic sauce called *daqqus* (also spelled *dakkus* or *dakoos*), and a yogurt relish to cool the palate after the spicy food.

HOSPITALITY

Most entertainment in Kuwait revolves around eating. Food and hospitality are inseparable for most Muslims and Arabs, and Kuwaitis are no exception to this rule. Hospitality is a vital part of both the old Bedouin code and a Muslim tradition, which requires the faithful to welcome guests with great generosity. Lavish dinners and lunches at home are the most usual form of socializing for families and friends.

MANNERS AND CUSTOMS

Before eating, most Kuwaitis say "*Bismillah*," which means "in the name of God." Afterward they thank God for such a good meal. In modern Kuwaiti homes, food is usually served at dining tables with cutlery and china. Many dining tables can seat twenty or more people. Men and women eat together

A produce grocer sits with his fruits and vegetables at an old souq in Al Qibla.

in cities, unless unrelated male guests are present. For large parties, men and women often eat and entertain separately so that the atmosphere can be more relaxed. The host always ensures that a guest has plenty to eat and his plate is never empty. It can be difficult for the guest to decline when full without offending the host, who might assume that the guest is unhappy with the food.

BEDOUIN DINING

More traditional people and particularly Bedouin may eat sitting on rugs and cushions on the floor, using low tables or a tablecloth spread on the floor. They sit with one leg tucked in beneath them and the other leg with the knee raised so that they can rest their arms on the knee. Men and women eat separately, with the women sometimes eating after the men have finished the choicest morsels. The diners share common serving dishes, from which they eat with their fingers, having previously washed their hands. Only their right hand is used to eat, and only from that part of the dish closest to them. Pieces of large loaves of flat bread, baked on a convex tray placed over a fire, are used to pick up the food and soak up the sauces.

Bedouin food was, by necessity, very simple. Milk and milk products, such as yogurt, remain a major part of the diet, which also includes grains such as wheat, dates, and very little meat. Animals are more useful for their milk than as meat. The only time some Bedouin would eat meat was when a sheep or a camel was slaughtered to celebrate a special occasion. Foods such as soups, rice, and seeds are enriched by the addition of clarified butter. To clarify butter, the butter is heated and then cooled; the clear yellow liquid that is strained off the top is the clarified butter, which can be kept in a tin. Fruits and vegetables, other than dates, were rare in the traditional Bedouin diet, as it is not possible to grow such things in the desert.

A nomadic Bedouin girl drinks camel's milk.

HALAL OR HARAM?

Muslims are not to eat pork, venison, or any animal that died a natural death. These are *haram* (har-AHM), or forbidden. For an animal to be fit for consumption, the person killing it must use a sharp knife to cut its throat while invoking God's blessings (*bismillah*), and it must be drained of its blood. It is then *halal*, allowed.

The products of haram animals must be avoided in other food, such as cookies and ice cream. For some Muslims, shellfish such as shrimp are considered haram. But this has not traditionally been so in the Gulf countries, where they are part of the diet. Alcohol in any form is forbidden, as is handling it or remaining in a place where it is sold or consumed. In Kuwait, alcohol is banned completely, which is not to say that some Kuwaitis do not drink it secretly at home.

TYPICAL MEALS

Breakfast is usually eaten early, as work and school usually start before 8 a.m. It consists of sweet tea or coffee, bread, honey or jam, and dates. Depending on the season, lunch or dinner is the largest meal of the day. Lunch is traditionally followed by an afternoon nap, due to the heat of the afternoon. Dinner is eaten late, when the evening cools down. Kuwaitis can stay up late and still rise early in the morning before the worst of the heat, since they take an afternoon nap.

Meals usually start with a variety of appetizers, which are also known as *meze*, many of which are common to the rest of the Arab world. These may include hummus, a smooth dip made with chickpeas and tahini, a paste of dried sesame seeds, garlic, salt, paprika, and lemon juice. Other popular appetizers include *falafel* (deep-fried bean croquettes), *warak al-inab* (stuffed vine leaves), and *samboosa* (pastries filled with meat, vegetables, and cheese).

The main course often consists of fish, sometimes chicken or lamb, and rarely beef. *Machboos* (called kabsa in some other countries), often referred to as the national dish, is a labor intensive dish of lamb, chicken, or fish cooked in a spicy broth and served over basmati rice.

As a food forbidden to Muslims, pork is never served. Fish is an important element in Kuwaiti cooking, and there are many ways of preparing it. Meat, chicken, and fish are served fried, stewed, stuffed, and barbecued as kebabs. Fish is often served in a curry sauce, as in India.

For very special occasions, Bedouin dishes such as camel meat and whole, stuffed baby lamb cooked in milk are prepared. Rice is a staple of all main courses, often served decorated with almonds and raisins and flavored with meat or fish stock, saffron, and spices.

Desserts are very sweet and not usually served after a meal but as a snack at other times. Common desserts include Turkish baklava, layers of very thin pastry and nuts bathed in a sweet syrup made of sugar and rose water. Almonds, pistachios, walnuts, raisins, cardamoms, rose water, and saffron are common ingredients of desserts.

Sweet baklava bites are a favorite snack.

FAST FOOD KUWAITI STYLE

Pizzas, hamburgers, and fried chicken are popular, especially among young people. Fast-food outlets are becoming places for both socializing with friends and family outings. But fast food is unlikely to replace traditional family dining, as Kuwaitis are very attached to dining at home with friends and family. Although Pizza Hut offers pepperoni pizza, there is one difference from the American version: beef pepperoni, made locally to taste just like the pork version, is used.

Kuwaitis also have their own traditional fast foods, and stalls and small shops in all areas sell kebabs, appetizers, ice cream, and juices. Sandwich bars are also popular and serve both American sandwiches and Arabic foods such as falafel.

Fresh fruits may be served after meals, usually chilled and beautifully prepared for the guests. It would be inhospitable to have guests cut up their own fruits. Refreshing fruits such as watermelons are often served after the afternoon nap. Dates are very popular.

FOOD PREPARATION

Because many Kuwaiti dishes require lengthy preparation—but mostly because Kuwaitis can afford it—most houses employ foreign servants to help with the cooking, serving, and cleaning up. Many Kuwaiti women will cook much of the food themselves but delegate the arduous preparation to servants. The tastes and styles of the foreign servants have influenced the nature of Kuwaiti cooking greatly, making it spicier and more varied than the food of most other Arab countries.

Many Kuwaiti houses have two kitchens: one inside for preparation, snacks, tea, and coffee, and one outside, which is ideally situated far from the living quarters. This is where lengthy and hot baking and other cooking are done. Much Kuwaiti food has a very strong smell, and the heat generated from cooking is most unwelcome in the hot climate. Kuwaitis try to keep their houses a cool refuge from the scorching streets.

For people who do not have an outside kitchen, most neighborhoods have small cooking shops. Manned by just one person and owned by immigrants, these kitchens specialize in preparing hot dishes, especially fish, according to the customer's instructions. These shops are now part of all planned housing developments. Once a fish is purchased at the market, it can be taken to this shop, where the spices to be used will be discussed. After about an hour, a phone call from the shop will let the customer know the fish dish is ready for pick up.

In a rural region of Kuwait, a mother bakes bread in an outdoor kiln.

INTERNET LINKS

https://delishably.com/meat-dishes/Widely-Eaten-Food-in-Kuwait
This site presents some of the favorite foods and flavors of Kuwaiti cuisine.

http://www.safaritheglobe.com/kuwait/culture/food-drinks
This travel site includes dining etiquette in its overview of Kuwaiti foods.

ARAB STYLE LAMB AND RICE

A true *machboos* is a complicated dish. This is a much simpler version.

2 tablespoons (30 grams) butter
1 pound (450 g) finely chopped or ground lamb
1 ⅓ cups (255 g) long grain white rice (Basmati is
   recommended)
2 ⅓ cups (555 milliliters) boiling chicken broth
1 ½ teaspoons salt
½ tsp black pepper
½ tsp allspice
½ tsp nutmeg
¼ tsp cinnamon
¼ tsp saffron (optional)
⅓ cup (50 g) lightly toasted pine nuts (pignoli nuts)
⅓ cup (50 g) golden raisins, soaked in hot water

Melt butter in a skillet or Dutch oven. Lightly brown the lamb meat in the butter. Add salt and spices and stir for 2 minutes.

Add the rice and stir; then add the boiling chicken broth and mix well.

Bring to a boil, cover, and simmer for 20—25 minutes or until rice is tender and liquid is absorbed. Stir in pine nuts and drained raisins.

Serve with plain yogurt if desired.

GERS OGAILY (KUWAITI SPONGE CAKE)

2 cups (230 g) all purpose flour
1 ½ tsp baking powder
¼ tsp salt
4 tbsp toasted sesame seeds
½ tsp saffron
1 tbsp sugar
4 eggs
1 ½ cup (300 g) fine sugar
½ cup (113 g) butter, melted and cooled
1 cup (250 ml) milk, room temperature
1 tsp cardamom
1 tsp rosewater

Preheat oven to 350 degrees Fahrenheit (180°Celsius).

Butter and flour the sides and bottom of a 10-inch (25 centimeter) Bundt cake pan, or a 9-inch (23 cm) springform pan. Set aside.

In the mortar, crush the saffron threads with 1 tsp of sugar until it becomes a powder. Add 2 tablespoons milk to the saffron powder. Leave to soak for at least 10 minutes.

In a large bowl, sift together the flour, baking powder, salt, and two tablespoons of sesame seeds. Set aside.

In the bowl of a stand mixer fitted with the whisk attachment, whisk the eggs and sugar on high speed until light, thick, and frothy, and about triple in volume—about 10 minutes.

In a large measuring cup, combine the butter, milk, cardamom, rosewater, and saffron mixture.

Gently fold the dry and wet ingredients into the eggs, beginning and ending with flour. Pour into the prepared cake pan. Sprinkle with the toasted sesame seeds.

Bake for 35 to 40 minutes, or until a skewer inserted in the middle comes out clean.

Cool completely on a wire rack before inverting.

Serve with tea.

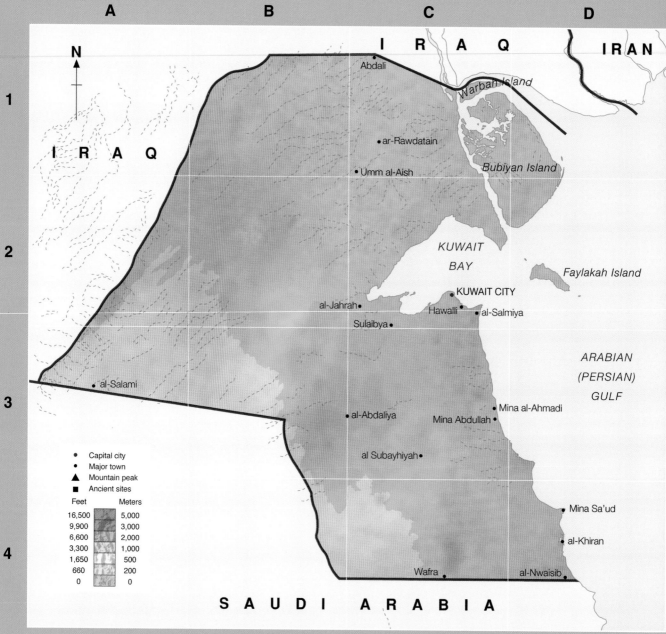

MAP OF KUWAIT

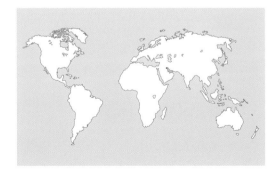

ECONOMIC KUWAIT

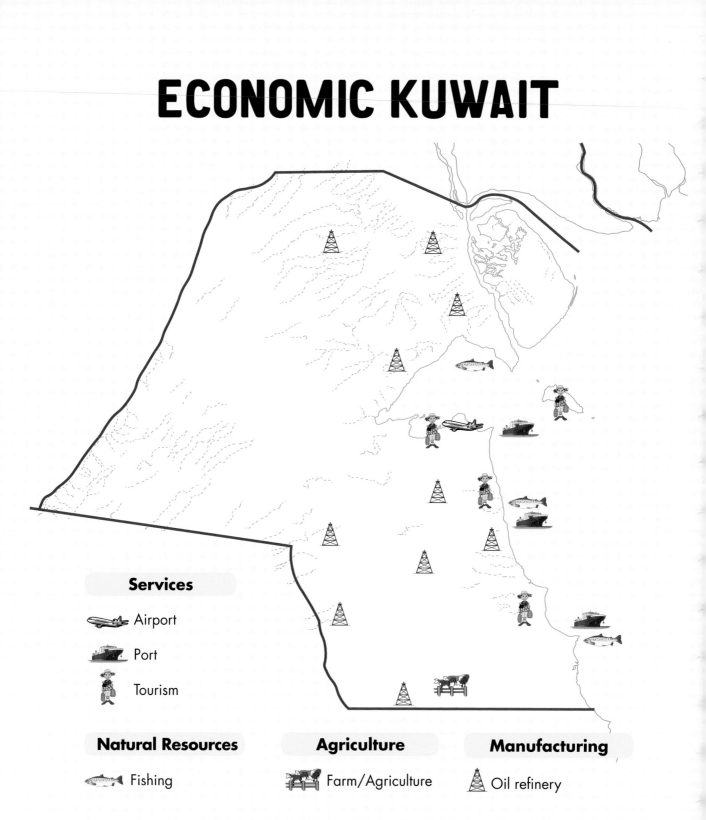

ABOUT THE ECONOMY

GROSS DOMESTIC PRODUCT
(official exchange rate)
$118.3 billion (2016)

GDP PER CAPITA
$69,700 (2017)

GROWTH RATE
—2.1 percent (2017)

LABOR FORCE
2.695 million; non-Kuwaitis represent about 60 percent of the labor force (2017)

UNEMPLOYMENT RATE
2.1 percent (2017)

CURRENCY
Kuwaiti dinar (KWD)
USD1 = 0.30 Kuwaiti dinar (KWD)
(January 2018)

MAIN EXPORTS
Oil and refined products, fertilizers

MAIN IMPORTS
Food, construction materials, vehicles and parts, clothing

MAIN TRADE PARTNERS
China, South Korea, United States, UAE, Japan, Germany, Singapore, and others

AGRICULTURAL PRODUCTS
Fish

INDUSTRIES
Petroleum, petrochemicals, cement, shipbuilding and repair, water desalination, food processing, construction materials

OIL PRODUCTION
2.795 million barrels per day (October 2017)

OIL RESERVES
101.5 billion barrels (2017 estimates)

NATURAL RESOURCES
Petroleum, fish, shrimp, natural gas

CULTURAL KUWAIT

Grand Mosque (al-Masjid al-Kabir)
The largest of Kuwait's mosques opened in 1986 and boasts a minaret 243 feet (74 meters) high. The mosque can hold up to 5,000 worshipers in the main hall, with room for nearly 7,000 in the courtyard.

Bubiyan Island
Kuwait's only substantial nature reserve is to the north of the country and is home to plentiful local marine life and coastal animals.

Failaka Island
Famed as the ancient Greek settlement of Icarus, this small offshore island at the mouth of Kuwait Bay is one of the most significant archaeological sites in the Gulf and home to temples dedicated to Artemis and Apollo. Once an important ancient trading post on the route from Mesopotamia to India, Failaka is undergoing development to turn it into a modern tourist resort.

Liberation Tower
Situated in downtown Kuwait City, the tallest building in the city at 1,220 feet (372 meters), it is thought to be the fifth-highest communications building in the world. The tower was completed in 1993 and celebrates Kuwait's liberation from Iraqi occupation.

Kuwait Towers
Housing a two-level revolving viewing deck, Kuwait's most distinctive landmark offers superb views of Kuwait City, the bay, and the Gulf beyond.

Scientific Center Aquarium
Housed in a spectacular sail-shape building on the cornice of Kuwait City, this is the largest aquarium in the Middle East and home to local species of crocodiles, giant spider crabs, mudskippers, turtles, desert hedgehogs, and living reefs.

Kuwait National Museum
Thel museum includes more than 20,000 artifacts from throughout the Arab world, as well as ancient treasures from Faylaka Island. After recent restoration work, the collection is back to being one of the best in the Middle East.

Green Island
This artificial island is joined to the mainland with a pedestrian causeway and is home to gardens, a lagoon, an amphitheater, a children's park, and cycle paths. It is also used as a launch pad for firework displays on national holidays.

Kuwait House of National Memorid
This modern museum bears testimony to the horrors of the Iraqi occupation, recording the experiences and sacrifices of ordinary Kuwaitis and the coalition forces that helped free the country in 1991.

Sief Palace
The official seat of the emir's court, this L-shape building dates from the early twentieth century and is an outstanding example of traditional Gulf architecture.

ABOUT THE CULTURE

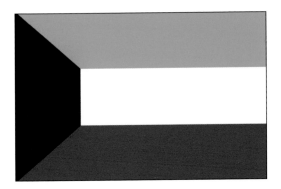

OFFICIAL NAME
Dawlat al Kuwayt (State of Kuwait)

NATIONAL FLAG
Three equal horizontal bands of green (top), white, and red with a black trapezoid on the hoist side; the design, which dates to 1961, is based on the Arab revolt flag of World War I.

NATIONALITY
Kuwaiti

CAPITAL
Kuwait City

LAND AREA
6,880 square miles (17,820 square km)

POPULATION
4,437,590, with immigrants accounting more than 69.5 percent (2017)

ADMINISTRATIVE AREAS
Six governorates: al-Ahmadi, al-Asimah, al-Farwaniyah, al-Jahra, Hawalli, Mubarak al-Kabir

LANGUAGE
Arabic (official), English widely spoken

ETHNIC GROUPS
Kuwaiti 31.3 percent, other Arab 27.9 percent, Asian 37.8 percent, African, 1.9 percent, other, 1.1 percent (includes European, North American, South American, and Australian) (2013)

RELIGIONS
Muslim (official) 76.7 percent, Christian 17.3 percent, other and unspecified 5.9 percent
Note: these figures represent the total population, of which 69 percent are immigrants.

BIRTHRATE
19.2 births per 1,000 population (2017)

INFANT MORTALITY RATE
7 deaths/1,000 live births (2017)

DEATH RATE
2.2 deaths/1,000 population (2017)

LIFE EXPECTANCY AT BIRTH
Total: 78.2 years
Male: 76.8 years
Female: 79.6 years (2017)

LITERACY
Total: 95.7 percent
Male: 96.4 percent
Female: 94.5 percent (2016)

TIMELINE

IN KUWAIT	IN THE WORLD
1700s	
Settlers from the interior of the Arabian Peninsula arrive at the site of present-day Kuwait City	
1756	
Kuwait comes under the control of the al-Sabah family.	**1789–1799** The French Revolution
1899	
Kuwait becomes a British protectorate.	**1914** World War I begins.
1937	**1939** World War II begins.
Large oil reserves are discovered by the US-British Kuwait Oil Company.	**1945** The United States drops atomic bombs on Hiroshima and Nagasaki.
1961	
Kuwait becomes independent and joins the Arab League.	
1963	**1969** US astronaut Neil Armstrong become first person to walk on the moon.
Elections held for National Assembly under terms of the newly drafted constitution.	
1976	
The emir suspends the National Assembly.	
1980	
Iran-Iraq War: Kuwait supports Iraq, giving its larger neighbor money to conduct the war.	
1981	**1986** Nuclear power disaster at Chernobyl in Ukraine
The National Assembly is recalled.	
1990	
Iraq invades and then annexes Kuwait over an oil dispute. The emir and cabinet flee to Saudi Arabia.	
1991	**1991** Breakup of the Soviet Union
US-led aerial bombing campaign begins in Kuwait and Iraq in January. Iraqi forces set fire to Kuwaiti oil wells.	
1993	
The UN draws a new Kuwait-Iraq border.	**1997** Hong Kong is returned to China.

IN KUWAIT	IN THE WORLD
	2001 9/11 terrorist attack on New York and Washington, DC
2003 US-led military campaign to oust Iraqi leader Saddam Hussein begins.	**2003** War in Iraq begins.
2005 Women gain the right to vote and run for office. The first woman cabinet minister, Massouma al-Mubarak, is appointed.	
2006 The emir, Sheikh Jaber III al-Ahmad al-Jaber al-Sabah, dies. Sheikh Sabah IV al-Ahmad al-Sabah is sworn in as emir.	
2008 Radical Islamists gain seats in parliamentary elections.	**2008** US elects first African American president, Barack Obama.
2009 Three women win seats in Kuwaiti parliamentary elections. Court rules Kuwaiti women can obtain passports without the consent of their husbands.	
2011 Hundreds of young people demonstrate for reform, inspired by "Arab Spring" protests.	
2013 Mussallam al-Barrak is sentenced to five years in jail for insulting the emir.	
2015 Sunni extremist carries out suicide attack on Shia mosque, killing 27 worshippers. Seven people are sentenced to death in connection with the attack.	**2015–2016** ISIS launches terror attacks in Belgium and France. **2017** Donald Trump becomes US president. Hurricanes devastate Houston, Caribbean islands, and Puerto Rico.
2018 Murder of Filipina maid highlights abuse of expat workers.	**2018** Winter Olympics in South Korea

GLOSSARY

abaya
A black cloak worn by women that covers the head and clothes.

bidoon (be-DOON)
Person denied Kuwaiti citizenship for lack of proof that his or her parents or grandparents were born in Kuwait.

burka
A mask that covers the face and body, worn by women.

bushiya (boosh-ee-YAH)
A black cloth covering the face.

dhow
Traditional Kuwaiti wooden boat.

dishdasha
Long robe worn by Kuwaiti men.

diwaniya (dee-WAHN-ee-yah)
A social gathering, usually for men, where business and politics are discussed.

gatra (GAT-rah)
Scarf worn by men to cover their heads.

hajj
The pilgrimage to Mecca prescribed of Muslims at least once in a lifetime.

halal
Food that Muslims are permitted to consume.

haram (har-AHM)
Food forbidden to Muslims.

hijab
Islamic hair or head covering for women.

oud
Arab stringed instrument similar to a guitar.

Ramadan
The month of fasting and extra prayer for Muslims.

sadu (sa-DOO)
Traditional Bedouin weaving.

salat (sal-AT)
Muslim requirement of praying five times a day in a prescribed manner.

saum (sowm)
Fasting between sunrise and sunset during month of Ramadan.

Sayyed
A descendant of the prophet Muhammad.

shahada (sha-ha-DAH)
Professing faith.

sirwal (seer-WAHL)
Long white trousers worn by men.

Sunni
The branch of Islam to which the majority of Muslims belong.

thob (thohb)
A long, loose dress.

zakat (za-KAAT)
Giving alms to the needy or to good causes.

FOR FURTHER INFORMATION

BOOKS

Al-Nakib, Farah. *Kuwait Transformed: A History of Oil and Urban Life*. Stanford, CA: Stanford University Press, 2016.

Atkinson, Rick. *Crusade: The Untold Story of the Persian Gulf War*. New York: Houghton Mifflin Co., 1993.

Hawley, Thomas M. *Against the Fires of Hell: The Environmental Disaster of the Gulf War*. New York: Harcourt, 1992.

Herb, Michael. *The Wages of Oil: Parliaments and Economic Development in Kuwait and the UAE*. Ithaca, NY: Cornell University Press, 2014.

ONLINE

Al Jazeera. "Kuwait News." http://www.aljazeera.com/topics/country/kuwait.html

BBC News. "Kuwait Country Profile." http://www.bbc.com/news/world-middle-east-14644252

CIA World Factbook. "Kuwait." https://www.cia.gov/library/publications/the-world-factbook/geos/ku.html

Encyclopedia Britannica. "Kuwait." https://www.britannica.com/place/Kuwait

Government of Kuwait. https://www.e.gov.kw/sites/kgoEnglish

Gulf News, "Kuwait." http://gulfnews.com/news/gulf/kuwait

Kuwait Times. http://news.kuwaittimes.net

Lonely Planet, "Kuwait." https://www.lonelyplanet.com/kuwait

New York Times, The. Kuwait archives. https://www.nytimes.com/topic/destination/kuwait

MUSIC

Ensemble Al-Umayri. *The Sawt in Kuwait*. Navras, 2003.

Various artists. *Music from the Arabian Gulf*. Arc Music, 2007.

Various artists. *Persian Gulf Expressway*. Naqmeh Banafsh Andisheh Cultural Institute, 2007.

FILMS

Fires of Kuwait. Warner Brothers, 1992. DVD release, 2001.

History Channel Presents: Operation Desert Storm. A&E Television Networks.

Lessons of Darkness by Warner Herzog. Shout! Factory, 1992.

BIBLIOGRAPHY

Arab Times. "Divorce Rate in Kuwait Reaches an Alarming 60 Percent This Year—'Interest-Driven Marriages'." May 22, 2017. http://www.arabtimesonline.com/news/divorce-rate -kuwait-reaches-alarming-60-percent-year-interest-driven-marriages.

BBC News. "Kuwait Country Profile." http://www.bbc.com/news/world-middle-east-14644252.

CIA World Factbook. "Kuwait." https://www.cia.gov/library/publications/the-world-factbook /geos/ku.html.

Fahim, Kareem. "Immigrant Maids Flee Lives of Abuse in Kuwait." *The New York Times*. August 1, 2010. http://www.nytimes.com/2010/08/02/world/middleeast/02domestic.html.

Freedom House. "Kuwait Freedom of the Press." https://freedomhouse.org/report/freedom -press/2016/kuwait.

Hegazi, Farah. "The 1991 Kuwait Oil Fires and Their Impact on Human Health." *Muftah*, February 21, 2017. https://muftah.org/health-kuwait-oil-fires.

Killius, Rolf. "Sing, Play and Be Merry: The Unique Sawt Music of the Arabian Peninsula." Qatar Digital Library. https://www.qdl.qa/en/sing-play-and-be-merry-unique-%E1%B9%A3awt -music-arabian-peninsula.

Kohn, Sebastian. "Stateless in Kuwait: Who Are the Bidoon?" Voices, Open Society Foundations, March 24, 2011. https://www.opensocietyfoundations.org/voices/stateless- kuwait-who-are-bidoon.

OPEC Annual Statistical Bulletin 2017. http://www.opec.org/opec_web/static_files_project /media/downloads/publications/ASB2017_13062017.pdf.

Oxford Business Group. "Kuwait Moves to Overhaul Health Care System." June 26, 2016. https://oxfordbusinessgroup.com/news/kuwait-moves-overhaul-health-care-system.

Sayed, Faraan. "A Few Surprising Facts About the Arabic Language." *Voices*, British Council, December 18, 2015. https://www.britishcouncil.org/voices-magazine/surprising-facts -about-arabic-language.

Toumi, Habib. "Kuwait Has World's Highest Water Consumption." *Gulf News*, April 25, 2011. http://gulfnews.com/news/gulf/kuwait/kuwait-has-world-s-highest-water -consumption-1.798870.

Trade Arabia. "$3bn Kuwait Causeway on Track for 2018 Opening." March 9, 2017. http://tradearabia.com/news/CONS_321732.html.

Villamor, Felipe. "Philippines Bars Citizens From Working in Kuwait After Body Is Found." *The New York Times*. February 12, 2018. https://www.nytimes.com/2018/02/12/world/asia /philippines-kuwait-duterte.html.

World Economic Forum. "Global Gender Gap Report 2017." http://reports.weforum.org/global -gender-gap-report-2017.

INDEX

INDEX